# THE CASE FOR HEAVEN

## Also by Lee Strobel

YOUNG
READER'S
EDITION

# THE CASE FOR HEAVEN

Investigating What Happens
After Our Life on Earth

# LEE STROBEL

with Jesse Florea

ZONDER**kidz**

ZONDERKIDZ

*The Case for Heaven Young Reader's Edition*
Copyright © 2022 by Lee Strobel

Requests for information should be addressed to:
Zonderkidz, *3900 Sparks Dr. SE, Grand Rapids, Michigan 49546*

ISBN 978-0-310-77017-6 (hardcover)
ISBN 978-0-310-75161-8 (audio)
ISBN 978-0-310-77018-3 (ebook)

Library of Congress Cataloging-in-Publication Data

*Cover Design: Diane Mielke*
*Interior Design: Denise Froehlich*

*Printed in the United States of America*

22 23 24 25 26 / LSC / 10 9 8 7 6 5 4 3 2 1

For Nabeel Qureshi—
I'll see you on the other side!
—LS


*To Joshua Mathis and the Mathis family. Your faith speaks volumes for the hope of heaven and the amazing reunions that await those who believe.*
—*2 Corinthians 4:16–18*
—JF

# CONTENTS

# HOW CAN WE KNOW THERE'S A HEAVEN?

One way or another, you're going to die.

I know what you're thinking: *What a gloomy way to begin a book for kids!*

And you're correct. After all, who wants to think about death?

Right now, you're more focused on all the things you look forward to doing in life. But just like you have a day you were born, there will come a day when you die. It's a fact of life. And when you slip from this world, what do you think you will find?

Nothing?

Or a reality that's more vivid, more exhilarating, more rewarding, and more *real* than anything you've ever known?

Many young people have different thoughts and beliefs about heaven. Which of these statements rings most true to you?

- Heaven is a place where we all become angels, sit on clouds, and play harps.

- Everyone goes to heaven because God is good and loving.
- There is no heaven. When you die, you just become worm food.
- One day God will create a new heaven and a new earth where his followers will live with him forever.

As you read this book, you'll discover if there's truth in any or all of those statements. And you'll learn about and wrestle with many other thoughts about the afterlife.

Maybe you've never thought much about heaven. Most kids haven't. But at the moment you transition out of this life, nothing will be more important to you. And if it will matter so much *then*, don't you think it's worth investigating *now*?

## The Evidence for Eternity

Years ago, I used my legal training and journalistic background as a prize-winning reporter to investigate whether there was any credibility to the Christian faith. At that point in my life, I didn't believe in God and hoped to discover there was no proof for his existence.

But the opposite happened. After two years of researching the work of the best scientists, historians, researchers, and scholars, I concluded there's persuasive evidence that Jesus indeed is the unique Son of God. Christianity is true! That's when I wrote *The Case for Christ*, a book that's sold more than five million copies.

Since then, I left my career as an investigative journalist to tell others the truth I had learned about God. Over the years I've taught at churches, appeared on TV shows and videos, and written more than forty books that dig into the claims of the Bible.

The Bible paints a vivid, beautiful picture of heaven. Scripture and Christian theology present heaven as the ultimate home for those who believe in God. But until a recent medical scare left me fighting for my life in the hospital, I never really studied whether there was specific evidence or compelling logic to support belief in heaven.

After recovering from my medical trauma, I decided to embark on a quest to get answers about the afterlife. I traveled to South Bend, Indiana, and Portland, Oregon. I went from San Antonio, Texas, to West Palm Beach, Florida, and beyond to sit down with scholars and quiz them about what they knew about this all-important matter.

Not only did I discuss heaven with these experts, we talked about so much more:

- Do humans have a soul that can survive our body's demise?
- What do personal stories of near-death experiences reveal about our future?
- Does physics, history, and philosophy provide insights about our existence beyond this world?
- How does Jesus, the one who was dead and came back alive a few days later, shed light on the subject?

I wanted to know whether spending forever in a blissful paradise makes rational sense. And who gets to go to heaven anyway? Some Christians believe even our pets will be there. And how about the awful reality of that "other place"? If the

Bible is right about heaven, its description of hell must also be true.

I also explored alternatives to the Christian worldview—for instance, reincarnation and the tenets of Islam. Billions of people follow those teachings. So I wanted to learn what belief system is the most believable and backed up by the most evidence.

Face it, there's a lot of controversy about life after death. Ask a bunch of random people about heaven, and three out of four will say they believe in heaven as a place where good people will be eternally rewarded.[1] But only half of people believe they'll end up in heaven.[2]

Wouldn't you want to be more confident than that? Batting .500 is great in baseball. But leaving yourself with a fifty-fifty chance of spending forever in misery doesn't sound like a good decision. You want to be 100 percent confident of your future when you die.

Truly, there's no more important question to look into than your belief in what happens after death. After all, if there really is an afterlife, you'll be spending a lot more time there than on earth. So shouldn't you investigate this issue sooner than later?

And think about how your life might change today—your priorities, decisions, actions, and worldview—once you look into the facts and confidently conclude what awaits you once your time in this world ends.

So come with me on a path of discovery. Consider the evidence. Evaluate the logic. Pursue the truth with an open mind. Then, in the end, reach your own informed verdict in the case for heaven.

# Cross-examination

In a court case, cross-examination is where hard questions can be asked. That's because important subjects deserve to be dug into and discussed—and your belief about heaven is one of those subjects. Regardless of where you find yourself on your spiritual journey, take time in this section to cross-examine the evidence about the afterlife.

The questions at the end of every chapter are meant to help you privately reflect on what you've read. But they can also be used to create conversations with a pastor, parent, or trusted adult in your life. Ask questions. Find answers. Build a foundation for what you truly believe will happen in the future.

**1.** As you begin this book, where are you on your spiritual journey on a scale of 1–10? Put an X on the line where you rate yourself.

| 1 | 5 | 10 |
|---|---|---|
| Don't believe in God | Just came to Christ | Fully faithful to God |

Why did you choose that number? What would it take for you to move farther up the scale?

**2.** If you could ask God one question about the afterlife and you knew he would give you an answer right now, what would you ask him?

**3.** This introduction previews many topics this book will cover: fear of death, the existence of the soul, near-death experiences, evidence for Christianity, heaven, and hell. Which of these issues are you most interested in reading about? Why?

# CAN WE LIVE FOREVER?

**1**

One day, you'll live forever as a brain floating in a glass jar.

At least that's what you might believe if you watch enough science fiction movies or cartoons. But these fictional depictions of immortality aren't too far off from experiments and testing that's happening today.

Billionaire inventors are experimenting with implanting computer chips into the human brain to extend life.[1] One Russian billionaire is working to create a digital copy of a person's brain. By replicating someone's personality, memories, and thought processes into technology, it would make it possible to live forever as an avatar or robot. [2]

For thousands of years, humans have been looking for ways to live longer. World-conqueror Alexander the Great searched for a healing river to extend his life. Alexander added lands to the Greek empire, but he couldn't add any days to his life. He died at age thirty-two in 323 B.C. Spanish explorer Ponce de Leon famously searched for the fountain of youth in Florida in the early 1500s. If he found it, it didn't work. Ponce died at forty-seven.

These days, people don't search for youth in magical springs of water. They look for it in science.

Author and scientist Aubrey de Grey says death is simply a medical problem. He and other scientists are working on antiaging medicines, cracking the genetic code, and creating treatments to delay death. De Gray believes the first person to live to one thousand years old is already alive today.[3]

Currently, the oldest man to ever live was Methuselah. The Bible says he lived to 969 (Genesis 5:27). That's a lot longer than today's average life expectancy of around eighty years.

Methuselah was the great-great-great-great-great grandson of Adam, the first man God created. At the beginning of the Bible, people often lived more than nine hundred years. Some Bible experts believe people lived longer back then because it was right after God made his perfect world. He designed humans to live longer, but disobedience brought death. When Adam and Eve sinned, it created a countdown on their lives. From then on, people have lived fewer years.

The Bible reveals that after the flood in Genesis 6–9, people didn't live as long. The next few books in the Old Testament show people's lifespans were very similar to what they are today. Even Moses lived to only 120, which is two years *less* than Jeanne Calment—a French woman who died in 1997 at the age of 122.

To learn more about people's desire to cheat death and live forever, I flew to Orange County, California, to talk with Clay Butler Jones. This author, leader, and professor has defended the truth of Christianity against experts from other religions. He's not afraid of writing and speaking about difficult topics. One of his most recent books is titled

*Immortal: How the Fear of Death Drives Us and What We Can Do About It.* And that's exactly what I wanted to discuss with him.

Our conversation stretched into several hours as we explored how the fear of death drives humanity, and how achieving immortality—of any sort—is pursued by so many people.

## Search for Immortality

"One way that people try to achieve immortality is to figure out how to live longer and longer in order to cheat death," I said.

I asked Clay about futurologists who talk about uploading our minds into a machine or scientists who study how improving our diets or finding new ways to fight diseases might add years to our lives.

Clay sighed. That's something I appreciate about him. He doesn't hide his feelings. He's a straight shooter who cuts to the core of the truth with his comments.

"If scientists were able to cure all cancers, people would only live an average of 2.265 years longer," he said. "A Harvard demographer [a population scientist] computed this. It doesn't matter—we'll die of something else. And when it comes to uploading our mind into a computer so we can be avatars in a virtual world or transferred into a robot . . . of course it's science fiction."

Clay told me, "As one expert explained, emulating the brain on a computer isn't the same as actually making a brain." He pointed out there are almost a thousand *trillion* connections in the human brain. That's a massive amount that computers can't even come close to duplicating.

Scientists also don't have the ability to figure out all of the brain's secrets. They can't even reproduce the brain of a small roundworm that has only 302 neurons—the human brain has 100 *billion* neurons! Clay added, "Another expert said even if artificial intelligence did 99 percent of the work, it would take a thousand years to map the brain."

He then said, "Even if we could produce something that's wired exactly like your brain, nobody has any idea how such a system could be conscious. Scientists can't explain how nonconscious stuff becomes conscious. And it's your consciousness that's the real *you* of your identity."

I went on to ask Clay about *cryonics,* which involves freezing a person after they die and then thawing them out once science has found a cure for what killed them. Some famous people have already had themselves frozen in hopes of living again. Theoretically, someone could continue this process of freezing and unthawing to live forever.

Again, he pointed out many problems.

"For one thing, you have to be frozen within a couple of minutes of dying or else your brain deteriorates," Clay said. "That's not very practical. Second, there's sonic fracturing."

To demonstrate the trouble with sonic fracturing, Clay reached over and poured some soda over the ice cubes in my half-empty glass. The ice made tiny cracking sounds.

"That's what happens if you try to thaw a brain or organ—*crack, crack, crack,*" he said. "Nobody knows how to fix that fracturing. One cryonics company actually suggests the possibility of sewing or gluing parts back together. Now you've got Frankenstein!"

*Wow!* I thought. *Nobody would want to live as a monster, even an immortal one.*

## Death Without God

After all of his research and study, Clay concluded that there's no way to avoid death. Once Adam and Eve decided to disobey God's command and follow their own desires to be like gods themselves, it brought death into the world.

"God has determined that people are going to die," Clay said. "Hebrews 9:27 says that 'people have to die once. After that, God will judge them.' We all *will* die. The big question, then, becomes how to make sure we spend eternity with God."

Clay's last comment hit at the core of my quest. Not only was it the *big* question, it was the biggest question of all! *How can we make sure to spend eternity with God?*

The Bible points to a clear path to eternal life. When Jesus walked the earth, he said, "I am the way and the truth and the life. No one comes to the Father except through me" (John 14:6).

Then after Jesus was killed, buried, and rose from the dead, his friend Peter stood in front of the teachers of the law and declared, "You can't be saved by believing in anyone else. God has given people no other name under heaven that will save them."[4]

This was the same Peter that months before had denied knowing Jesus as he was falsely accused and taken to the cross.[5] Now Peter was boldly proclaiming the truth that Jesus Christ of Nazareth was nailed to the cross, rose from the dead, and was the only way to heaven. Something changed Peter's actions. He went from scared to strong. And that *something* was seeing the risen Jesus Christ.

Of course, not all people believe in Jesus. Countless

other philosophies and beliefs exist. Many of these start with the idea that there is no God.

"The quest for a salvation without God is at the heart of every great philosophical system, and that is its essential and ultimate objective," Clay said, quoting a French philosopher.[6] In other words, many philosophies try to find a way of dealing with death *without* God.

"Much of philosophy is trying to conquer the fear of death," Clay continued. "Philosophers, anthropologists, psychologists, sociologists, psychiatrists—they're fascinated with how death affects behavior."

Some philosophers argue that the idea of death motivates individuals to work, build, and accomplish great things. Because time is limited, people want to make the most of it. Many social scientists say the fear of death drives culture.[7]

Clay agrees with the idea that the fear of death motivates people to act. If death is always approaching, we feel compelled to do something with the time we have on earth. However, Clay was quick to point out that we don't have to be afraid of dying. He read Hebrews 2:15, where it says Jesus can set people free who are afraid of death.

"Scripture confirms that we are in bondage to a fear of dying," Clay said. "Jesus came to rescue people. If people don't follow Jesus, who's going to free them of that dread? They've got to somehow find a way to free themselves—and that leads to all kinds of problems."

Those problems can include depression and denial. Atheists deny the existence of God. They try to convince themselves that nothing happens after death. Because they believe they don't have an eternal soul that lives on, they act like death is no big deal. It's like they think, *I lived. I died. Whatever.*

In Clay's book, he summed up the atheistic view of death without God this way: "When you die, your consciousness will cease. Your body will then decay where, as *The Hearse Song* goes, 'The worms crawl in, the worms crawl out / the worms play pinochle on your snout.' You have no hope of reuniting with loved ones. You will never again enjoy other people, or sunsets, or beaches, or breakers, or mountains, or redwoods, or roses, or anything else for that matter."[8]

*Talk about bleak and hopeless,* I thought. *No wonder people get depressed.*

## Hope for Eternity

"But if Christianity is true—and we have good reasons to believe it is—then we face judgment after death," Clay continued. "We don't face the nothingness of nonexistence; instead, we either face an eternity with God or separated from him. That's the *real* truth about immortality."

The Bible says after followers of Christ pass from this world, they rejoice in God's presence. They're reunited with loved ones, living without tears or struggles or fears. Heaven is a wondrous world of adventure, excitement, and exploration. We live with contentment, joy, and love—*forever.*

Our lives are precious. We need to make the most of our time on earth. But in the timeline of eternity, our lives are over in the blink of an eye.

Clay had made it clear that death is inevitable. We can't deny that it'll happen to us. There's really no room for false hope in medicine. Wishful thinking that science can defeat death doesn't work. Our empty efforts to somehow achieve eternal life apart from God always fail.

It was time to end my conversation with Clay and search for further evidence that our death in this world can be an actual gateway to a more fabulous forever existence. Many questions still had to be answered: Was there scientific evidence of the existence of the human soul? And what might heaven look like?

For now those questions would have to wait. I wanted to look more into the fear of death. Clay had pointed out that the fear of death motivates many of our actions. Was that a good thing or bad thing? And is death something to be feared at all?

To find answers, I needed to visit an old friend. And that meant jumping on a plane and flying up the Pacific Coast to Portland, Oregon.

**1.** If you could live forever as a brain in a jar, as a robot, or in heaven, which would you choose? Why?

**2.** Think about life without God. Does that scare and depress or excite you? Why do you think people come up with philosophies that try to explain the universe without God?

**3.** On a scale of 1–10, put an X on the line to represent how afraid you are of dying.

| 1 | 5 | 10 |
|---|---|---|

| Petrified! | Don't think about it | Not afraid at all |

**4.** Have you ever discussed the topic of death with your family? Do you have any questions for them right now? Write some down.

# IS DEATH SOMETHING TO FEAR?

**2**

What do you fear?

Researchers have found little kids are afraid of monsters and scared that it will hurt when they go to the bathroom.

You've probably overcome those fears. But the world can be a scary place. Older kids often fear bad people hurting them or getting a long-term illness. Some are afraid of heights, amusement park rides, and icky spiders. The most common fears, however, include being rejected by friends and the fear of death.[1]

The fear of death is hard to escape. And if it's scary for you, don't you think it'd be worse for an eighty-five-year-old man who's close to dying?

To answer that question, I flew to Portland, Oregon, to spend the day with Luis Palau Jr. Born in the 1930s, he and the ministry he founded have shared the good news about Jesus with a billion people worldwide. Yes, you read that right—a *billion*.

Not only did Luis speak at large churches and stadiums in seventy-five nations, he thrived in face-to-face ministry.

Whether it was the Hispanic busboy at a Mexican café or the young clerk at a grocery store, Luis took every opportunity to share the life-changing forgiveness and hope that's only found in Jesus.

I'd known Luis for more than thirty years when I learned he had stage 4 lung cancer. Doctors expected him to die in less than a year. He surprised them by living more than three years and continuing to serve God and spread biblical truth. I'd always admired Luis' passion for Jesus, the accuracy with which he spoke from the Bible, his fearless proclamation of the gospel, and his emphasis on the love of God.

Luis died on March 11, 2021, surrounded by his family. When I visited his home a few months before that, his family was there too. I could tell his energy was lagging, but nothing could dim the enthusiasm in his voice as he spoke about what the Lord had done and what was to come.

## No Fear of Death

Most people don't like to talk about death. But Luis knew why I'd come. He was ready to have the conversation.

"Do you fear death?" I asked.

"No," he said quickly, then he paused briefly. "No," he repeated, more emphatically this time. "I don't really. I'm so convinced from Scripture that after I close my eyes for the last time, I go to be with God. The apostle Paul says that to be absent from the body is to be present with the Lord."[2]

The apostle Paul, the greatest evangelist of all time, also said, "To live is Christ and to die is gain" (Philippians 1:21, NIV). Being with God isn't something to be feared—it's something to look forward to. For Christ followers, our forever home is heaven. But that doesn't mean we won't be missed or miss certain things on earth.

When Luis first received his cancer diagnosis in 2018, he thought about what he'd miss most. That was easy; it was his family. He wouldn't be able to pick up the phone and talk to his sons. He wouldn't be able to have conversations with his wife.

Instead of traveling the world, he spent his last few years more connected to his family and more at peace in delighting in God.

"I read the Bible with very open eyes," Luis told me. "Every mention of heaven is underlined in green, with a little dot. I've started visualizing *me* seeing the great throne of God, *me* walking the glorious streets, *me* reuniting with those who have gone before."

Luis couldn't wait to see the face of Jesus. He wanted to talk with his dad again. (Luis' father died when Luis was a ten-year-old boy.) He looked forward to speaking with heroes of the Christian faith and seeing the throne of God.

Revelation 4 gives a mind-blowing description of God's throne. It's a passage Luis had read many times before my visit. He described to it to me from memory: "The One sitting on it has the appearance of jasper and ruby. There's a rainbow shining like an emerald; there are flashes of lightning and peals of thunder; there's a sea of glass, clear as crystal. Twenty-four elders and fantastic creatures, along with a heavenly host, are praising the Lord."

Luis then said, "How much of that is literal? How much is a word picture to point us toward something we can't even comprehend at this point?" He paused and smiled. "Well, I can't wait to find out."

## A Call for All

Luis also anticipated spending time with his mother. He recalled when he was a new Christian in Argentina that his mother urged him to take the gospel to nearby towns that didn't have a church.

"She kept encouraging me and pushing me," he said. "She'd say, 'Go, go, go. Get out and reach people with the good news!' But I was slow to step out in faith. I'd say to her, 'Mom, I'm waiting for the call.'"

His mom didn't like that reply. She got upset and said, "The call? The *call*? The call went out two thousand years ago, Luis! The Lord's waiting for *your* answer! You're not waiting for *his* call!"

Luis knew she was right. The Bible makes our task clear—go out and reach people with the truth and love of Jesus. Whether they're friends, family members, neighbors, classmates, or just people we meet along the path of life, everyone should hear about Jesus. The assignment for every believer is to spread God's love. There's no excuse for inaction.

"I'm guessing your mother's words got you moving," I said.

"It was one of the defining moments of my life," Luis answered. "I realized I didn't need to wait around; instead, I needed to *do*."

Luis did *do*. During his sixty years of ministry, God used him to bring at least a million people into a saving knowledge of Jesus Christ. That's an amazing number—and one that amazed Luis.

"If I've ever impressed anybody, I hope it's because they

realize I'm not very special," he continued. "I hope they say, 'If God can use an ordinary person like Luis, why can't he use me?' You don't have to be a genius. You can just be a boy from a small town in southern Argentina. And if we're faithful, the sky's the limit—because the power comes from God."

That's his encouragement to fellow believers: Trust in God's power and go for it! Step out in faith, take action, strike up a conversation with someone about God. It's the Holy Spirit's job to convict people of their sin. We can't control whether someone accepts the gospel. But as Luis told me, "We can bring them the best news on the planet—that there's redemption, there's a relationship with God, there's heaven, and there's an eternal party waiting for them."

Will everyone immediately believe that truth? No. Could you be rejected and made fun of for your commitment to Christ? Sure.

"But when all is said and done," Luis said, "you'll never regret being courageous for Christ."

## Hope of Heaven

By living a courageous life for Christ, Luis didn't fear death. His hope was in heaven. Luis pointed to Hebrews chapters 7–10 as powerful Scriptures that affirm Jesus came to earth to do away with sin. His sacrifice covered every sin and shortcoming. And Jesus still goes before God the Father to intercede for those who believe in him.

"Jesus is defending us," Luis said firmly. "If you put your trust in the Lord, your salvation is secure. This theme of 'once for all' is stressed repeatedly in Hebrews. Through

Christ's sacrifice on the cross, *all* of our sins are atoned for—paid in full—finally, completely, for all time."

For example, Hebrews 7:27 says with crystal clarity, "Jesus gave one sacrifice for the sins of the people. He gave it once and for all time. He did it by offering himself."

While Luis didn't fear his own death because he knew his ultimate home was in heaven, he recognized that death can be scary because many people are on the path to hell.

"I haven't shied away from the bad news that our sin has separated us from God and so we're headed for hell," Luis said. "But the good news is that Christ offers forgiveness and eternal life in heaven if we repent and follow him. People need to hear that positive and uplifting message.

"The Bible says it's God's *kindness* that leads to repentance,"[3] he added. "He sets us free! What's better than that? Our relationship with God can be full of joy and laughter and happiness."

I had one last question for a man who'd spent his life telling others about God's kindness, love, forgiveness, and goodness.

"What about people who aren't yet Christians?" I asked him. "If you could send them a message after you go to heaven, what would it be?"

Luis didn't mince words. "I'd tell them, *'Don't be stupid!'*"

We both burst out laughing. "Seriously?" I said. "That's *it*?"

"Sure," he said. "Don't be stupid! Don't pass up what God is offering out of his love and grace. Why turn your back on heaven and choose hell? Why expose yourself to the harmful side effects of a sinful life when you can follow God's path of righteousness and healing? Don't miss the party that God has waiting for you in heaven!"

Somehow, when I had gotten on the plane to talk with one of the world's most renowned evangelists, I didn't expect our conversation to end with him simply saying, "Don't be stupid."

Then again, nobody wants to be stupid.

We don't want to blindly follow a faith that's not based on fact or put our trust in something that's not true. At the same time, we certainly don't want to miss out on what is promised to be the greatest gift—and greatest party—of all time due to a lack of faith or overreliance in scientific theory.

I still had a lot of questions to be answered. Did Luis' belief in his eternal soul living forever with God make any scientific sense? I wanted to research if there is any compelling evidence that people possess a "spirit" that can continue to endure after we take our last breath in this world.

Recently, I had heard about a Cambridge-educated neuroscientist who might be able to provide solid answers. Though she lived all the way over in England, technology enabled us to connect for an in-depth interview.

**1.** What are your top fears? How do you deal with things you're afraid of?

**2.** Besides God, who are the top three people you'd like to meet in heaven? Why did you choose these individuals?

**3.** Luis Palau said he read the Bible with "open eyes," knowing that he'd soon be in heaven. What do you think that means, and how can you follow his example when you read God's Word?

**4.** Luis said his message from heaven to non-Christians would be, "Don't be stupid!" If you're a Christ follower, how do you react to his advice? Do you agree, or does that sound too harsh? If you're not a Christian, are you offended? Challenged? Encouraged? What are your emotions?

# DO WE HAVE A SOUL?

**3**

I f an alligator eats a mouse, what happens to the mouse? Can it run, hear, eat, and play?

If you said no, you'd be correct. When an alligator eats a mouse, the mouse ceases to exist.

Psychologists asked this same question to kids between four and six years old. They showed these young children an illustration of an alligator eating a mouse and said, "Well, it looks like Brown Mouse got eaten by Mr. Alligator. Do you think the mouse's ears still work?"

While the kids understood the mouse was no longer alive, and therefore it couldn't hear or run, they still believed the mouse had thoughts and desires. In other words, the mouse's body may have been wiped out, but it had a spirit that kept going on.[1]

Researchers concluded this study demonstrates children naturally believe that living things have both a body and a soul. While the body can die, the soul lives on. Throughout history, many great thinkers and philosophers have supported the idea that people are both body *and* spirit.

Our bodies are skin and bone, muscles and organs. Our

"spirit" brings life to the body. The body can be seen. The soul can't. The soul is the source of our personality, emotions, desires, memories, perceptions, and beliefs.

The exact word *soul* appears more than forty times in the NIrV translation of the Bible.[2] As an example, in one of the most famous prayers in the Old Testament, Moses tells the Israelites to "love the LORD your God with all your heart and with all your *soul*. Love him with all your strength" (Deuteronomy 6:5, italics added). When Moses gave the people this command, he used the Hebrew word *nephesh*, which was translated into English in this verse as "soul." But nephesh has a bigger meaning. In Hebrew, it describes our whole being or person. It's *all* of us. And that's how God wants us to love him—with *everything* that we are.

The writers of the Bible also used the Hebrew word *ruach* (frequently translated as "spirit") and the Greek word *psyche* (generally translated "soul") to talk about the soul. In Greek, *psyche* refers to the invisible "entity" that directs our physical bodies. *Ruach* most often refers to the "breath of God" that sustains all living things. And these words occur hundreds of times in the Bible. But since experts on the Bible can't always agree on whether those words definitely refer to the soul each time they appear, the only thing we know for sure is that the Bible doesn't *directly* teach us about what the soul is and whether it exists.

Of course, that doesn't mean the Old and New Testaments don't support the belief the soul is indeed real. Many verses using these words show humans are made of both a spirit and a body that work together to make up our whole being. Philosopher and professor J. P. Moreland put it this way when talking about himself: I *am* a soul, and I *have* a body.[3]

J.P. has studied all the different references to the soul in Scripture and written about his findings. In one of his books, he writes, "In Matthew 10:28, Jesus warns us not to fear those who can only kill the body; rather, we should fear Him who can destroy both body and soul." In this warning, Jesus affirms the reality of the soul. From the clues that J.P. pieced together from different verses, he says the Bible

## What's the Intermediate State?

When believers in Jesus die, they go to heaven. That's a true statement promised in the Bible. Christians will spend eternity in a new heaven and a new earth that God creates after Jesus returns (see Revelation 21). So what happens from the time between a person's physical death and Jesus' return?

Bible experts use the term *intermediate state* to describe this temporary existence of our spirits between death and the final resurrection. When I use *intermediate state* in this book, it refers to this period of time. This is a time of pure happiness in the presence of God. It's the place that Jesus called "paradise" when he hung on the cross (Luke 23:43). We won't be bored or impatiently waiting for "heaven." It may be referred to as *intermediate*, but it'll be awesome.

When you read the word *heaven* in this book, know that I'm using it to describe the new heaven and the new earth where followers of Jesus will live for eternity in their forever bodies with God after judgment occurs.

You'll read a deeper explanation of heaven and the intermediate state in chapter 5, "What Is Heaven Really Like?"

teaches that our soul separates from our body at the point of death as we enter into a temporary *intermediate state*. We're in the presence of God, but we receive our indestructible resurrection bodies at the end of history when Jesus comes back and God creates the new heaven and earth.[4]

While the belief in the soul dates back thousands of years, some scientists are now saying that human beings are just a brain. These scientists argue that we don't have a soul. They say we're only electrical impulses that fade to nothing when we die.

So what's the truth? Is it reasonable to believe that our consciousness, or soul, continues to exist in an afterlife? Or are we simply physical brains that are snuffed out when our heart stops pumping and our brain waves flatten?

To find out, I decided to interview a neuroscientist who has conducted brain research in Britain and the United States.

As a child, Sharon Dirckx (rhymes with *lyrics*) always wanted to be a scientist. Church wasn't a big deal for her family in Durham, England, so she grew up thinking science and God didn't go together.

During her first week at the University of Bristol as a teenager, she attended a meeting that featured a panel of knowledgeable Christians. "They made the case that of course a person can be a Christian and a scientist at the same time," Sharon said. "It rocked my world."

She ended up spending the next eighteen months investigating Christianity and came to a saving faith in Jesus when she was twenty. Sharon then earned an undergraduate degree in biochemistry and a doctorate in brain imaging at Cambridge University.

Her 2019 book *Am I Just My Brain?* made a compelling case for why the answer to her book's title is [spoiler alert!] a gigantic *NO*.

## Going Beyond the Physical Brain

After connecting with Sharon via video over the internet, I started with my first question: "You've used high-tech imaging machines to peer inside human brains. Did you see a soul?"

"I wasn't looking for one," Sharon replied with a smile. "As a neuroscientist, I was studying things like the effects of drug addiction on the brain. That's what scientists do—we explore the physical world. Some people assume science can do more than it really can. For instance, it's not designed to resolve the question of whether God exists. Of course, if God is real, there will be signs pointing in his direction—as I believe there are."

I agreed. From the wonders of nature to planetary orbits, and from the Earth's tilt to the intricacies of the human eye, God's design and handiwork are everywhere. I've interviewed experts and written about the evidence of God's existence in my other books, including *Case for a Creator for Kids*.

As science continues to advance, researchers are discovering truths that we could never see in the past, such as the secrets of human genetic code and how atoms are bonded together. With all of this new knowledge, I asked, "If science can't prove that God exists, can it prove that God doesn't exist?"

"It's important to point out that the recent discoveries

of neuroscience are *entirely* compatible with the existence of God," she said. "Science could never disprove God. That would be like scientists figuring out how all the programming works on Facebook and then declaring, 'So this disproves the existence of Mark Zuckerberg.'"

Now it was my turn to smile. "You're saying that science can tell us many things, but we still need philosophy and theology."

She nodded. "The Bible says that God has made himself known in two ways—through the natural revelation of the physical world and the special revelation of Scripture. Science tells us a lot about the natural world, but we still need theology and philosophy to explore special revelation—the Scripture—and to give thought to questions that science cannot answer. Questions like 'Why can we *think* at all?'"

Sharon explained how scientists *can* measure brain activity. They see networks in the brain light up when various thoughts take place. But those networks aren't the thoughts themselves. Scientists cannot access a person's *actual* inner thoughts without asking them what they're thinking.

"A person's thoughts defy traditional scientific methods," Sharon added. "As a neuroscientist, I've measured the electrical activity of people's brains, but I can't measure their experience in the same way. I can't measure what it's actually like to be *you*." She pointed toward me and smiled. "You, Lee, are more than just your brain."

She then provided additional evidence that humans are more than flesh and bone. In her book, Sharon tells the story of Pamela Reynolds. In 1991, this woman suffered a severe brain bleed. She was rushed into surgery. In order to save her life, doctors cooled her body temperature, "flatlined" her heart and brain signals, and drained the blood from her head. Clinically, Pamela was dead. But when she was resuscitated after the surgery, she astounded everyone by saying she had been conscious the whole time.

"When a person dies, their consciousness should be extinguished—right?" Sharon asked. "But what if near-death experiences [called NDEs, like Pamela had during surgery] show that we can still be conscious without a functioning brain? Again, that would demonstrate that human consciousness is more than just physical brain activity."

Thousands of patients have told stories about being clinically deceased and yet floating out of their body and watching resuscitation efforts from above. Many have described traveling through long tunnels, seeing deceased relatives, and experiencing an astoundingly beautiful realm beyond our world.

Personally, I had never explored the question of whether NDEs are credible, so I asked Sharon, "Do you think NDEs can provide good evidence for a soul and an afterlife?"

"There have been studies conducted in the United States, the Netherlands, and elsewhere," she said. "Some of the stories have very intriguing evidence."

She went on to say that if there was just *one* documented case of someone dying and yet staying aware of what was happening in the room, then it would deal a serious blow to the idea that consciousness resides entirely in the brain.

"It would also suggest that even the sciences point to evidence of an afterlife," she added.

I made a mental note to look into the credibility of NDEs as Sharon continued to build her case that people have souls that live on when our brains stop.

## Made for Another World

"Human beings are highly complex," she said. "The implication that we are just our brains is incredibly limiting."

Sharon noted that people are made from many parts. "We don't just have a brain. We have a personality, we have genetics, we experience trauma, we have a certain upbringing—all kinds of things [like experiences and biological factors] shape our minds and who we are." From our fingerprints to the way we think, each person is unique.

For her next point, Sharon reached into her extensive study of the Bible. She speaks around the world, defending the truth of the God's Word against other worldviews.

"The Bible says that human beings were made in God's image," she said. "Consequently, it makes sense to say that because God has a mind, we have a mind; because God thinks, we think; because God is conscious, so are we." Sharon also noted, "It also explains why we sometimes long for more than this world. Human beings aren't temporary, but we are intended to live on for eternity." Our desire to have an eternity is because God created us to live forever and have a relationship with him. And we are relational as well. Which means God wants to know us, and we deep down want to know him.

With that, she stressed her conclusion: "Actually, that's the ultimate point of consciousness: *so that we can know God.*"

For me, the case had been made. I am more than just skin and bones. To go back to J. P.'s statement from earlier in this chapter: I *am* a soul, and I *have* a body. That conclusion opens the door to the possibility that when my body takes its last breath in this world, I can actually live on.

I picked up Sharon's book and read the end: "Christianity says you are more than your brain—you are made for eternity. One way or another, there will be consciousness in eternity, either with Christ or apart from him. Live today with eternity in mind."[5]

Death is not the end. Eternity awaits because we live on through our soul. The first building block in the case for an afterlife was in place. Still, there was more evidence to consider.

What about near-death experiences? Could they really shed light on what happens after we die? There are scholars who think so, including prominent Christian philosopher Paul Copan from Palm Beach Atlantic University, who I planned to talk to later.

First, I wanted to speak with someone who had researched and written a book about the credibility of NDEs or out-of-body experiences. To find those answers, it meant a trip to Austin, Texas.

**1.** After reading this chapter, how convinced are you that humans have a soul that lives on? Put an X on the line to represent your belief that the soul separates from our body at the point of death.

| 1 | 5 | 10 |
|---|---|---|
| No soul | Don't know what to believe | Sold-out for the soul |

**2.** As a kid, Sharon Dirckx started asking big questions like, *Why can I think? Why do I exist? Why am I a living, breathing, conscious person who experiences life?* Have you personally wrestled with thoughts like this? How would you answer those questions?

**3.** Sharon went away to college thinking scientists can't believe in God. Have you ever heard that opinion? Does it make sense to you based on the fact scientists study God's creation?

# CAN WE PEEK INTO LIFE BEYOND DEATH?

## 4

Seven-year-old Katie couldn't wait for the birthday party at the local swimming pool. She had just learned to swim and wanted to test out her new skills. But at the party, disaster happened.

After being bumped by some older boys, Katie found herself floundering in the deep end of the pool. She fought to stay afloat but ended up under the water.

Minutes later, Katie was found lifeless and floating face-down in the swimming pool. She was profoundly comatose, with massive brain swelling and no measurable brain activity. For nearly twenty minutes, she didn't have a heartbeat. Amazingly, she was resuscitated and taken to the hospital, where Dr. Melvin Morse began treatments.

When the doctor first saw Katie, he hooked her up to an artificial lung to keep her breathing. She stayed in a coma for three days. Dr. Morse thought Katie would die. And if she did come out of her coma, he was convinced she'd have irreversible brain damage.

Somehow, though, she made a miraculous recovery. Not only did she live, but she could talk, walk, and think just like before her accident. Stunned, Dr. Morse visited his patient and asked what she remembered about her experience. He figured Katie would tell him how she had tried to stay afloat in the pool. Instead she said, "You mean when I saw the heavenly Father?"

Katie went on to explain how when she was in the hospital, she left her comatose body and watched as the doctors and nurses tried to save her. Then she told how she went through a tunnel and met an angel who took her to her home, where she watched her brother play and her mom cook dinner. She could see them, but her family had no idea she was there.

"You'll see," Katie said when she ended her story. "Heaven is fun."

Intrigued, Dr. Morse questioned her for a long time. He had her draw a picture of the emergency room. She successfully drew everything in its correct place during the time she was unconscious. Then the doctor asked for specific details about what she observed when her spirit visited her home. Katie talked about what her father was reading, how her brother was pushing a toy soldier in a Jeep, and that her mother was cooking roast chicken and rice. She even knew what clothes each family member wore that night.

Dr. Morse asked her family about Katie's descriptions, and everything checked out exactly as she described.[1]

If humans are just a brain, as some people believe, how is a story like Katie's possible?

In my view, just like neuroscientist Sharon Dirckx said in the last chapter, all that's needed is *one* well-documented case of a near-death experience to prove we each have a soul that continues our consciousness after death.

I was looking for hard evidence based on real stories, and I knew who might have it. John Burke, a longtime friend of mine, has researched more than a thousand cases of near-death experiences and written two books on the topic: *Imagine Heaven* and *What's after Life?* I contacted my friend and set up an interview at Gateway Church in Austin, Texas, where he's the pastor.

I was hoping to find just *one* case. John gave me a lot more than that.

## View of the Afterlife

We sat down together in the conference room at Gateway Church, and I asked my first question. "In all of your research," I said, "what was your most surprising discovery about near-death experiences?"

"First, I'm not particularly fond of the term near-death experiences," he began. "As one survivor said, 'I wasn't *near* dead; I was *dead* dead.' Some of these cases involve people with no heartbeat or brain waves. There are instances where doctors had already declared them dead. They may not have been *irreversibly* dead, but many were certainly *clinically* dead."

"Okay, good point," I said.

"Now, let me answer your question," he continued. "What surprised me the most is that even though they vary a fair amount, these accounts have a common core—and incredibly, it's entirely consistent with what we're told about the afterlife in the Bible . . . The Bible contains black-and-white words about the afterlife, and these NDEs tend to add color to the picture."

The fact that these experiences complemented the Bible

surprised me a bit and also gave them more credibility in my mind. "What are some of the common traits in people's experiences that make you believe they line up with the Bible?" I asked.

John explained that three out of four people experience the separation of consciousness from their physical body. Their "spirit" leaves their body and sees things that would be impossible to experience on earth. Two out of three encounter a mystical or brilliant light. More than half describe unworldly or heavenly realms where they meet other beings—either mystical ones or deceased relatives or friends.

"Tell me more about the divine presence that people experience," I said. "What do people typically say about him?"

To answer this question, John told the story of Ian McCormack from New Zealand. Ian had grown up in a Christian home, but he didn't believe in God. One day Ian was scuba diving off the coast of Mauritius in the Indian Ocean when he was stung four times by box jellyfish.

I cringed. I knew from my travels that these jellyfish are often called the world's most venomous creature. One sting can result in death in two to five minutes.[2] And Ian was stung *four* times.

"Ian was dying," Burke said. "He saw visions of his mother, who had told him to call out to God if he ever needed help. He was in utter darkness and felt terrified. He prayed for God to forgive his sins—and a bright light shined on him and literally drew him out of the darkness. He described the light as 'unspeakably bright, as if it was the center of the universe . . . more brilliant than the sun, more radiant than any diamond, brighter than a laser beam. Yet you could look right into it.'"

John continued the amazing story, saying, "Ian said this

presence knew everything about him, which made him feel terribly ashamed. But instead of judgment, he felt 'pure, unadulterated, clean, uninhibited, undeserved love.' He began weeping uncontrollably. Ian asked if he could 'step into the light.' As he did, he saw in the middle of the light a man with dazzling white robes—garments literally woven from light—who offered his arms to welcome him. Ian said, 'I knew that I was standing in the presence of Almighty God.'"[3]

John paused and then continued. "Remember the transfiguration [when Jesus took some of the disciples up the mountain and showed them his true glory]? In Matthew 17:2, it says Jesus' face 'shone like the sun. His clothes became as white as the light.'" John smiled. "Reminds me of that."

I saw the similarities too. But Ian came from a Christian background, so he was familiar with images of God. Maybe his brain was just pulling from past experiences. So I asked, "What if Ian had grown up a Hindu? Could that have changed his experience? Maybe he would've 'seen' a god from that faith?"

John shook his head. "In all my research, I've never read of people describing anything like the Hindu gods Krishna, who has blue skin, or Shiva, who has three eyes," he said. "In fact, two researchers studied five hundred Americans and five hundred people from India to see how much their cultural conditioning may have affected their NDE."

"What did they find?" I asked, becoming even more interested.

"That several basic Hindu ideas of the afterlife were never portrayed in the visions of the Indian patients," John said. "No reincarnation. But they did describe encountering a white-robed man with a book of accounts. That's very consistent with what we find in the Bible."

"What about people who say these experiences are just hallucinations or caused when a person experiences extreme trauma or a lack of oxygen in the brain?" I asked.

John picked up his book and flipped through to find the pages that addressed this concern. He admitted that a lot of theories have been put forth over the years. However, a heart doctor from the Netherlands did a large-scale study of NDEs and concluded that physiological and psychological factors couldn't fully explain these experiences.

John quoted from his book, "His [the doctor's] bottom line was that these theories 'fail to explain the experience of an enhanced consciousness, with lucid thoughts, emotions, memories from earliest childhood, visions of the future, and the possibility of perception from a position outside and above the body.'"[4]

"There's still controversy about NDEs though, right?" I said.

"Certainly the debate continues," John answered. "An increasing amount of research is being done. More than nine hundred articles have been published in scholarly journals. But many skeptical researchers have now concluded that NDEs give us a peek into the afterlife. None of the alternative explanations make as much logical sense as the straightforward conclusion that there really is life after death."

## Look for the Red Sticker . . . and Missing Shoe

The consistent testimonies, changed lives, and stories of similar encounters reported around the globe was impressive. John had certainly done his research. But I was hungry for hard evidence. The investigative journalist in me wanted something that could be checked out.

"Are there cases where a person witnessed something during an out-of-body experience that would've been impossible for them to see otherwise?" I asked. "I'm looking for undeniable corroboration of a *fact*."

John's reply surprised me. "Oh, sure," he said. "Quite a few."

I leaned forward and got ready to take notes. "Give me some examples."

John began with a story of a woman in London, England, who went into Memorial Hospital with severe bleeding. As the blood drained from her body, she heard a *pop* sound and found herself inches from the ceiling, watching and hearing everything that was going on. She even noticed a red label on top of one of the ceiling fan blades. Then she floated into a place filled with radiant white light. Suddenly, she "popped" back into her body. After she told the doctors and nurses what she experienced, she convinced them to get a tall ladder and look for the red sticker hidden on top of the emergency room ceiling fan. When they looked, it was exactly as she described.[5]

"The part about the sticker in her story gives it a certain credibility," I admitted. And John wasn't done.

"One of the most famous cases comes from researcher Kimberly Clark Sharp, who describes the out-of-body experience of a heart-attack patient named Maria," he continued. "During the time Maria was unconscious, she drifted through the ceiling and outside the hospital. When she did, she saw a tennis shoe on the hospital's third-story window ledge."

"How did she describe it?" I asked.

"A man's shoe, left-footed, dark blue, with a wear mark

over the little toe and a shoelace tucked under the heel. Kimberly investigated, and sure enough—she eventually found the shoe, exactly as Maria had described it."[6]

I pondered his stories for a moment. "That's impressive," I said. "How often does this kind of corroboration occur?"

John cited a study of ninety-three patients who made multiple verifiable observations while out of their physical bodies. The research found that remarkable 92 percent of the observations were "completely accurate." Another 6 percent contained "some error." Only 2 percent were "completely erroneous." [7]

"That's pretty amazing," I said.

John then told me he knew of undeniably amazing real-life cases, where people who were blind since birth could see during their NDE.

He told the story of Vicki, who had never visually seen anything. She was twenty-two years old when she was in a car accident and found herself looking down on the crumbled vehicle. Later, she watched doctors working on her body as she floated toward the ceiling. After going down a tunnel to a wondrous place, Vicki saw a playback of her earthly years. When she revived, she was able to provide various accurate observations, including details about the appearance of childhood friends, which she could not have witnessed before due to her blindness.

## A Beautiful Picture

My time with John was nearly finished. He'd provided me with numerous documented cases of NDEs that included solid corroboration of the facts. And I knew this was just the tip of the iceberg. "So what do you want people to walk away with when they hear these stories?" I asked.

"Many people I've interviewed try to describe the astonishing beauty they've seen in heaven," John said. "Scenery that takes your breath away. A fragrance so gentle and sweet. Colors like nothing on earth. But then they say, 'Yes, it was amazing, but I didn't even care about it. Because I couldn't take my eyes off Jesus. He's beyond beautiful. He's everything I've ever longed for.'"

John's eyes met mine. "I want people to see that Jesus is everything we want," he continued. "Everything I've ever enjoyed in life—all of that is just a speck compared to the greater reality that's found in him."

I left the conference room and kept thinking about what John had said. The evidence he cited convincingly demonstrated that consciousness *does* continue after clinical death. These people could never have witnessed what they saw unless they'd had authentic out-of-body experiences.

In my mind, the best explanation for the totality of the evidence is that after our brain stops working, after our heart stops beating, after the doctors declare us dead—we still live on. Our consciousness survives. *We* survive.

Researcher Jeffrey Long—a doctor who uses radiation therapy to treat cancer—came to the same conclusion. After studying many of these experiences, he said, "NDEs provide such powerful scientific evidence that it is reasonable to accept the existence of an afterlife." [8]

But what is the afterlife like? Many of the descriptions John provided lined up with what I'd read about heaven. But there was so much more to uncover. What will happen in heaven? Will some people receive special rewards for the way they've lived? What will heaven really look like?

I couldn't wait to dig deeper—and I knew just where to go for more information. I reached out to a prominent New Testament scholar who has written about what he calls "the heaven promise."

He agreed to meet. And for that to happen, I'd need to go back to my old stomping grounds of Chicago, Illinois.

# Cross-examination

**1.** After reading this chapter, how convinced are you that humans have a soul that lives on? Put an X on the line to represent your belief that the soul separates from our body at the point of death.

| 1 | 5 | 10 |
|---|---|---|
| No soul | Don't know what to believe | Sold-out for the soul |

Did your X move between the last two chapters? Why?

**2.** Which NDE story in this chapter intrigued you the most? Do you believe the details provided are strong evidence that our consciousness continues after clinical death?

**3.** Why do you think seeing Jesus during their NDE amazes people more than their heavenly surroundings?

# WHAT IS HEAVEN REALLY LIKE?

**M**any ideas, myths, and misconceptions exist about heaven. Have you heard any of these?

- Everyone will live in cloud houses, have wings, and play harps.
- You'll enter through pearly gates, and there will be gold and diamonds everywhere!
- It's a never-ending church service. You'll sing songs to God and pray to him continually.
- You get everything you ever wanted—toys, ponies, remote-controlled helicopters, and more.
- It'll be like living in a huge mansion with lots of rooms.
- God will be there, as well as family and friends and pets, but no bad guys or pain or suffering.
- Heaven will be boring—you'll just do the same things over and over and over.

Well, there's some truth in *some* of those statements. But let me address the last one first.

Heaven will definitely *not* be boring. That lie about heaven was created by people who don't believe in God. To deal with their fear of death, they try to convince themselves that eternal life would be supremely boring because they'd run out of pleasurable things to do. Instead of giving their lives to a loving God who radiates light, they choose darkness.

I'll talk more about hell—the final consequence for this sad and disastrous decision—later in this book. But know that heaven isn't filled with endless repetition. You won't eat chocolate cake every day and read the same book over and over.

Clay Butler Jones, who I interviewed in the first chapter, said it best: "If heaven is real, then God will make all things new, and he will be continually creating a world of joy and wonder for us. If God can create all the beauty and excitement of our current universe, he's certainly capable of creating an eternally stimulating and rewarding experience for his followers in the new heaven and the new earth."

Clay's words reminded me of where it says in the Bible, "No eye has seen, no ear has heard, and no mind has imagined what God has prepared for those who love him" (1 Corinthians 2:9, NLT).

The truth is we won't know and can't know everything about heaven until we get there. But there are some facts we *can* know right now.

To dig into those facts, I traveled to a church in the northern suburbs of Chicago to talk with Scot McKnight. Scot's a respected New Testament scholar. His book on the afterlife, called *The Heaven Promise*, debunks several popular myths and sets the record straight on what we can truly learn about heaven from biblical accounts. Scot has spoken around the world, teaches at a seminary, and has written more than eighty books.

## A New Heaven and a New Earth

After greeting each other, I presented some of the thoughts people have about heaven from the list at the beginning of this chapter. Scot immediately recognized the fact that Jesus told his disciples that "there are many rooms in my Father's house" (John 14:2) and that Revelation 21:4 promises that there will be no crying, death, sadness, or pain in heaven.

But his eyes widened when he read through the misconceptions that heaven is some sort of ethereal existence, up in the clouds, where we are ghostly souls who spend every waking hour singing to God.

"There's a lot to set straight there," he said. "We need to see heaven in two phases. First, there's the present heaven, which is where we go when we die. This is a temporary situation—I liken it to a college dormitory where students don't expect to stay forever. Eventually, they'll move into a more permanent condo or house."

"This would be the so-called 'intermediate state,'" I offered.

"Correct," Scot said. "Jesus said to the thief on the cross, 'Today you will be with me in paradise.'[1] When Stephen was being stoned to death, he looked up to heaven, or paradise, and saw the glory of God.[2] We don't have a lot of information to go on, but in this intermediate state we will be consciously present with God. Ultimately, this present heaven is going to give way to a new heaven and a new earth. That's the second phase."

"So in the end, heaven isn't some far-off place in the clouds—it's *here*," I said.

"Right. It's the complete renewal of our world," Scot said. "It's a physical place, not just for spirits or souls, but for resurrected bodies designed for the kingdom of God. John says in Revelation 21, 'I saw "a new heaven and a new earth." The first heaven and the first earth were completely gone. There was no longer any sea. I saw the Holy City, the new Jerusalem. It was coming down out of heaven from God.'"

Scot explained how this world will resemble our present earth, but it will be a transformed place for transformed people.

"We're talking about a glorious redemption and restoration of all creation," he continued, his voice getting more animated. "Jesus described it as a place with multitudes of rooms for his followers. God will dwell with us, and we will dwell with God. We will actually see God's face. Can you imagine that? All of creation will be set free and turn to God in praise. It will be creation on steroids, the way it was designed to be, with celebrations, music and songs, festivals and festivities."

Seeing God. Having parties. Living in new bodies. There was a lot to unpack here. So I started with more questions. "What will we look like in this new heaven and new earth?" I asked.

"Our bodies will be transformed and imperishable," Scot said. "They will be perfected for a new kind of existence in eternity. It's important to note that this isn't a *new* body; it's a transformation of our *current* body. There's a one-to-one correspondence, or continuity, between the two. People in heaven will recognize us. They'll say, 'Hey, it's Lee Strobel!'"

I laughed. But I also thought of another question. "So what age will we look like in heaven?"

Scot admitted there have been long debates about that question. Some experts think it will be the age of Jesus at his resurrection, so around thirty-three years old. Nobody really knows because the Bible doesn't provide that specific detail. But Scot is confident that biblical texts show we'll recognize each other, be able to talk with each other, and continue to grow and learn.

He patted his bald head. "I'll even have hair in heaven," he added with a chuckle.

## Worship and Friendship

Scot had answered what we'll look like in heaven. "But what will we do in heaven?" I asked.

"Heaven will be a place of both worship *and* fellowship," he said. "It will be a glorious union of delight in God *and* delight in one another. We have a king *and* we will be citizens of his kingdom, who are in a flourishing society together."

That sounded great . . . but a little unrealistic. As Christians we're forgiven, but definitely not perfect. We hurt each other, get in arguments, stop talking to each other, and mess up in countless other ways. If we'll recognize each other in heaven, certainly these quarrels could carry over into eternity. With all of that in mind, I asked, "How will we fully enjoy ourselves in heaven if we're around people who hurt us while we were on earth?"

"That's a good question," Scot said. "I believe one of the first things that will happen in heaven is reconciliation. We'll have face-to-face meetings with everyone we've been in conflict with—and there will be truth telling, confession, honesty, and repentance. No excuses, no pretending. Friendships will be repaired; relationships will be set right; families will be reunited."

"Why do you think that?" I asked.

"How else can we carry on in peace and harmony if these rifts aren't healed?" he said, answering my question with a question.

Scot didn't know exactly how these relationships would be healed. Maybe it will happen immediately. But restoration and forgiveness must take place for heaven to be a place where there's no crying, sadness, or pain. And we will *want* it to happen. Here on earth, sometimes our pride or emotions get in the way of mending relationships. But in heaven, God will fill us with the desire and ability to reconcile with each other.

Scot paused to remind me that the Bible doesn't give us a high-resolution picture of every detail in heaven. Rather, it uses metaphors and images to fuel our imagination to picture what eternal life with God will be like. One such picture is Jesus preparing rooms for us in heavenly homes.

The Bible also contains several metaphors of banquets and feasts in heaven. In fact, the first image of the kingdom of God in the book of Revelation is a wedding celebration of love and friendship and community.[3] The church is often called "the bride of Christ." In heaven, we won't just have fellowship with each other. We'll have direct fellowship with God.

As Pastor John Burke alluded to in the last chapter, Scripture has several references to the hope of seeing God face-to-face in eternity. The apostle Paul said that although we see things dimly now, someday in eternity "we shall see face to face" (1 Corinthians 13:12). And Jesus said in the Sermon on the Mount, "Blessed are the pure in heart, for they will see God" (Matthew 5:8, NIV).

"This concept of being face-to-face with God seems a little confusing," I said to Scot. "In the Bible, God told Moses, 'You can't see my face, for no one may see me and live.'" [4]

Scot wasn't confused at all. "Yes, the Bible says people cannot gaze on God and survive his glorious brilliance," he said. "But while God's full presence is unendurable for humans here and now, in eternity all of his followers will get face time with him. When we're in heaven, we won't merely be able to *survive* his glorious presence, we will *revel* in [intensely enjoy and celebrate] it forever."

## Trustworthy and True

Now it was my turn to pause and put everything together. Heaven will be *here*, in this world, a re-created and renewed environment free from sin and decay. It'll be a bustling place full of friendships and beautiful nature and filled with the presence of God. We'll even see God face to face. What a staggering thought!

As the apostle John wrote in Revelation 21:5 (NIV), "He who was seated on the throne said, 'I am making everything new!' Then he said, 'Write this down, for these words are trustworthy and true.'"

We can know without a doubt that God's words are "trustworthy and true." But as Scot pointed out, the Bible often uses metaphors to help us picture what heaven will look like. Many times exact details aren't provided.

Without all the specifics, debates have raged through the centuries about *what* and *who* will be in heaven. There's a temptation to go beyond what the Bible says and use our imaginations to fill in the details. Instead of allowing my mind to go there, I jotted down some big questions I wanted an expert to answer.

And I just happened to be sitting in front of a world-class Bible scholar. I looked up at Scot. "I've got several more questions about heaven that I'm especially curious about," I said. "And I'm still looking for more biblical confirmation on why I should believe in heaven at all."

He motioned for me to continue. "I'll do my best," he replied.

**1.** After reading this chapter, put on X on the line to show how exciting you think heaven will be.

| 1 | 5 | 10 |
|---|---|---|
| Snoozeville | Just okay | Best party ever |

**2.** Scot said the Bible teaches heaven isn't some place where souls just float around, but it's a "new heaven and new earth." God's creation will be renewed and renovated. Christ followers will live forever in resurrected bodies like the one Jesus had after he rose from the dead.[5] Was that a new concept for you? What is your reaction to it?

**3.** Is there someone you would wince at seeing in heaven because you are currently mad at or afraid of them? What do you think it will be like to be reconciled with people who have hurt you? Would you look forward to it or would it concern you?

**4.** As you finished reading this chapter, what aspect of heaven are you still the most curious about?

# WHY SHOULD I BELIEVE IN HEAVEN?

# 6

Everyone at church said heaven will be great. Twelve-year-old Zayden wasn't so sure. He wanted to go to heaven. But living forever seemed sort of . . . scary. *What would it feel like?* he wondered. *Forever is a really loong time.*

Zayden talked to one of the pastors at his church in Phoenix, Arizona. Then he wrote into a popular Christian magazine to ask what he should do about his worries. A few months later, his letter appeared in the magazine, along with a response that acknowledged other kids also feared the unknown of what happens when we die.[1]

Zayden felt better knowing he wasn't the only kid who had questions about heaven. Talking with his pastor and hearing back from the magazine helped him think more about his future. He believed God created humans with physical bodies and eternal souls. Because of that, he knew his eternity could be spent *with* God or *apart* from God. The choice was his. Did he believe in a loving God who freely offered forgiveness through his Son, Jesus, or did he reject the existence of a heavenly Father?

That was an easy decision for him: *God all the way.* What wasn't easy was all the stuff he didn't know about the afterlife. To help him handle his fears of the unknown, Zayden decided to focus more on what he *did* know. He trusted that God loved him. He believed that Jesus died for him, forgave him, protected him, and had a plan for him. Even though he still didn't understand eternity, Zayden understood that God was good, so heaven would be good. He also liked what Jesus told his disciples: "Do not let your hearts be troubled. You believe in God. Believe in me also. There are many rooms in my Father's house. If this were not true, would I have told you that I am going there? Would I have told you that I would prepare a place for you there?" (John 14:1–2).

In the end, Zayden realized he wouldn't have all the answers this side of heaven . . . and he was okay with that. He would continue to follow God, learn more about heaven from the Bible, and talk with his parents, pastors, and other people to grow in his faith.

## Nine Reasons to Believe in Heaven

As I continued my conversation with Scot McKnight, I appreciated Zayden's desire to understand more about God and the future yet to come. We all want peace and confidence in what we believe, so I asked, "Why do you believe in heaven?"

Like any good theologian [someone who is an expert on God's teachings, faith, and religion], Scot laid out his thoughts crisply and systematically, saying he had nine reasons in all.

## Reason 1

"First, I believe in heaven because Jesus and the apostles did," Scot said. Then he pointed out four specific Bible verses to make his case.

- Jesus said in John 6:40, "My Father wants all who look to the Son and believe in him to have eternal life. I will raise them up on the last day."
- Later in the New Testament, Peter promised his churches they would "receive a rich welcome into the kingdom that lasts forever. It is the kingdom of our Lord and Savior Jesus Christ" (2 Peter 1:11).
- One Jesus' closest friends, the apostle John, who walked with Jesus for three years and was always by his side, said, "Here is what God has promised us. He has promised us eternal life" (1 John 2:25).
- The apostle Paul, who traveled the world telling people about Jesus and ultimately died because of the boldness of his beliefs, talked about our frail bodies, saying, "We know that the earthly tent we live in will be destroyed. But we have a building made by God. It is a house in heaven that lasts forever" (2 Corinthians 5:1).

"If all of them believed in heaven," Scot concluded, "then it's good enough for me."

## Reason 2

The second reason is because Jesus was raised from the dead. This isn't just something talked about in the Bible. Historians and others have written about Jesus—how his grave was empty, and how his followers said they'd seen him again.

"To me, that's the big one," Scot said. "Not only was Jesus resurrected, but people saw his body; they talked with him; they ate with him; and then he returned to the Father with the promise that he will come back."

This gives great credibility to an afterlife. As another famous New Testament scholar said, "The resurrection of Jesus is the *launching of God's new world*."[2] That new world will one day include the new earth and new heaven.

### Reason 3

"My third reason for believing in heaven is that the overall Bible believes in it," Scot said matter-of-factly.

"Wait a second," I said. "The earliest books in the Bible don't teach much at all about heaven."

Scot agreed that most of the statements about the afterlife in the Old Testament are found in the later books, but he also identified earlier verses that point to heaven or an intermediate place.[3]

There's the mysterious story of Enoch early in the book of Genesis. The Bible says, "Enoch walked faithfully with God. And then he couldn't be found, because God took him from this life" (Genesis 5:24). It's the first account of a person not dying, and instead being taken from this world to be with God. And it happened again with Elijah.

This great prophet of God "went up to heaven in a strong wind" (2 Kings 2:11). One minute, Elijah was walking with this friend Elisha. The next minute, a chariot and horses made of fire appeared and Elijah was taken up to be with God.

"Divine revelation unfolds over time," Scot continued. "The Bible's major themes develop and grow and expand. It's like watching a play, where the whole story isn't clear until the end. It's the New Testament, especially once we get to Jesus' resurrection, that ushers in a new hope for eternal life and heaven."

## Reason 4

"What's your fourth reason for believing in heaven?" I asked Scot.

"Because the church has taught it consistently," he said.

I knew this was significant. If the church had ever wavered on its teachings about eternal life or significantly altered its beliefs, it would mean relevant biblical passages were unclear or confusing. But these verses have been accepted and trusted by Christian scholars for two thousand years.

"Christian theology from the very beginning has believed in an afterlife, especially because of the resurrection," Scot said. "There has never been an era in which the church hasn't believed in heaven."

## Reason 5

Scot's fifth reason for believing in heaven surprised me.

"Because of beauty," he said. "Even atheists [people who don't believe in God] get awestruck by the grandeur of the world."

Whether it's visiting the Grand Canyon, strolling among the California redwoods, watching waves crash in the Pacific Ocean, or witnessing a sunset over the Rocky Mountains, God makes himself known in creation. Scot explained that the beauty of earth points us toward something beyond.

"Many of us believe in heaven because we see in the present world a glimpse of something far grander," Scot said. "Could it indicate a future reality—a new heaven and a new earth? If God made a world this good, doesn't it make sense he would make a world where it will all be even better?"

Scot let that question linger for a minute and then moved on to his next reason for believing.

## Reason 6

Most people believe in heaven. Scot cited statistics showing that 84 percent of Americans believe in some kind of heaven, with nearly seven out of ten convinced that it's "absolutely true."[4] Even with fewer people going to church, more people are believing in an afterlife.[5]

"Essentially, humans down through history and across different religions and philosophies have always believed in an afterlife," Scot said. "Why is that? Is there something built in to humans, a feeling from God, that there's life beyond the grave? The Bible says God has 'set eternity in the human heart.'[6] I believe the history of human belief in heaven is an argument for believing it's true."

## Reason 7

His seventh reason needed a little more explanation. "Because of desire," he said.

The things of this world don't satisfy. A famous story describes how the richest man in the world was asked what he wanted—how much money would satisfy? His answer was, "Just a little more." Even with more money than any human could ever need or spend, wealth didn't satisfy. He desired *more*.

Christian author and thinker C. S. Lewis once wrote, "If

I find in myself a desire which no experience in this world can satisfy, the most probable explanation is that I was made for another world."[7]

Scot explained that the "world" C.S. Lewis wrote about is heaven. "I believe that the ongoing lack of fulfillment in possessing what we desire—the love of another, family, beauty, work, wealth—indicates there is a true home that will ultimately satisfy all our desires fully," he said. "And that home is heaven."

## Reason 8

With that, Scot went on to his eighth reason for believing in heaven—our longing for justice.

"This world reeks of injustice," he said. "We've been told since childhood that life isn't fair."

He pointed in the direction of the city of Chicago, noting that life isn't fair for innocent kids who get shot. Racial discrimination isn't fair. It isn't fair that Christians around the world are thrown in jail, separated from their families, and even killed because they believe in Jesus. The rich seem to get richer while the poor people seem to get poorer. Criminals escape prison on technicalities. None of that is fair.

"We seem to have an innate sense of what's right and wrong," Scot said. "We long to see justice done. I believe in heaven because I believe God wants to make all things right. He wants justice to be finally and fully established." And it will be in heaven.

## Reason 9

That left one reason. "I believe in heaven because science doesn't provide all the answers," Scot said. "A lot of people believe scientific knowledge is superior to any other form of knowledge. But that's simply not true. Science can tell us how the world works and behaves, but it can't probe meaning and purpose."

As neuroscientist Sharon Dirckx pointed out in an earlier chapter, science can map brain function, but it can't know thoughts, explain consciousness, or understand love.

"The point is that science can't prove heaven, but not everything has to be subjected to scientific scrutiny," Scot continued. "For instance, we have excellent historical evidence for Jesus' resurrection, and that ought to be sufficient to point toward the reality of an afterlife with God."

The Bible also makes it clear that Jesus was "taken up to heaven" and the apostles watched until a cloud hid him from their sight (Acts 1:9).

## Most Asked Question

Scot had done an excellent job answering my first question, but I had several more—including the question I get asked most often about heaven. From everything I'd witnessed so far, Scot knew his stuff. But would he be able to answer my next questions?

## Cross-examination

**1.** Have you ever felt like Zayden—you believe in heaven, but you're sort of afraid to go there? How did you deal with your concerns about the afterlife? Are you still looking for more answers?

**2.** Of the nine reasons in this chapter, which one is your favorite? Did you find some of the reasons more persuasive than others? If so, which ones?

**3.** Write down what you think is the strongest evidence for the belief in heaven.

# WILL THERE BE PETS IN HEAVEN?

**7**

Images of heaven leap off the pages of the Bible. Walls made of rubies, sapphires, amethyst, and other precious jewels. Streets paved with gold. Amazing light shining everywhere.[1]

The new heaven and new earth will also be populated by all sorts of wildlife. The prophet Isaiah in the Old Testament wrote that "wolves will live with lambs. Leopards will lie down with goats. Calves and lions will eat together" (Isaiah 11:6). In the New Testament, we learn that Jesus will triumphantly return to earth riding a white horse. That means there must be horses in heaven. Lots of them, because the armies of heaven will also be riding horses (Revelation 19:11–14).

But what about kittens or hamsters, chinchillas or parakeets, dogs or pot-bellied pigs? Most families have a furry, feathery, or scaly friend that endears itself to kids and parents alike. Certainly we'd love to see them again in eternity, but what do the biblical facts say?

## Do All Dogs Go to Heaven?

I posed the question to Scot. "Our pets are warm and wonderful companions, but will we see them again in heaven?"

The Bible expert leaned back in his chair and smiled. Before answering the question, he told me about his childhood pet—a black Labrador named Sam.

"Sam used to go on my paper route with me," Scot said. "But he had the instinct of a retriever, so at first when I'd throw a newspaper in front of someone's house, he'd run after it and bring it back to me."

That made me laugh. I had fond memories of pets and how their personalities perked up my days.

Scot noted that some verses mention certain animals in heaven, but the Bible doesn't specifically address pets. However, that doesn't mean there's no possibility of pets in the afterlife.

Scot explained, "I'm convinced that heaven will not be a duller place than this world, and I think the world would be duller without pets."

"So you believe specific pets will greet us in the final heaven?" I asked.

Scot smiled and told a story of when famous theologian Richard Mouw was a kid and asked his mom if pets will be in heaven. Richard said that when he became a father years later, his son asked him the same question.

"In both cases, the answer was, 'Well, dogs don't have souls, you see. But anything is possible with God. He will do what is best for us.'"[2] Scot paused to stress his next words. "God will *always* do what's best for us. So while our focus in heaven won't be on pets, I believe it would be just like God to have our dogs there for us."

Many people agree with Scot. A survey of the oldest pet cemetery in America—where seventy thousand animals are buried—showed that before the 1980s almost no inscriptions mentioned any hope of seeing their pets in heaven. But since the 1990s, gravestones often "express the owner's belief in an afterlife for the pets, as well as the expectation, or at least the hope, that owners and pets will be reunited."[3]

And while science hasn't established that pets have souls, like humans do, studies have indicated that animals feel emotions. Elephants have been shown to grieve the death of a member of their herd.[4] Dolphins and whales seem to express happiness. (Maybe that's why dolphins always look like they have a smile on their face?) Parrots can become cranky. And barnyard animals such as pigs, horses, and cows can display characteristics of fear.

Because God created animals, the beauty, power, joy, and strength of his character can be seen in them. However, only humans were created in God's image. It was only after God created man that the Bible says, "It was very good" (Genesis 1:31).

Philosopher J. P. Moreland, who I quoted earlier talking about the human soul, believes our pets don't have complex souls like humans. But he says there is biblical evidence they may possess a more basic type of soul.[5]

When Christian thinker Peter Kreeft was asked about pets in heaven, he replied, "Why not?" He pointed to Psalm 36:6, which many Bibles translate as, "You save humans and animals alike, O Lord."

"We were meant from the beginning to have stewardship over the animals," Peter added. "We have not fulfilled that divine plan yet on earth; therefore it seems likely that the right relationship with animals will be part of Heaven. . . . And what better place to begin than with already petted pets?"[6]

Over and over again, Bible experts have said they wouldn't be surprised if pets were in heaven, because it would be keeping with the character of God. He's a giving and forgiving Father who is extravagant with his grace and blessings. Plus, God gives the best gifts.

- He gives us life.
- He offers us the free gift of eternal life.
- He gives us our family.
- He gives us wisdom.
- He gives us peace.
- He gives us joy that can't be taken away.
- He even gives us his Spirit to help us understand the truth of his Word.

So *why* not pets in heaven? We can't know for certain, but I agreed with Scot. God *always* does what's best for us!

With that question answered to my satisfaction, I moved on to the next one. It was something I'd heard debated about in church, so I wanted to hear what Scot had to say about the subject.

# Cross-examination

**1.** Would you rather have your favorite toy or favorite pet with you in heaven? (circle one)

**FAVORITE TOY**                              **FAVORITE PET**

Explain why.

**2.** The question about pets being in heaven is a big one for some people. Do you expect to see your pets in heaven? If they were there, what would that say about the character of God?

**3.** Do you believe God welcomes our questions, or do you think he is bothered by them? Why is it important to ask questions and then look for answers from reliable sources (i.e. the Bible, parents, grandparents, pastors, etc.)?

# WILL THERE
# BE REWARDS
# IN HEAVEN?

# 8

Do you like to win? Everybody does.

Whether it's in school, sports, board games, dance competitions, or video games, we all quest to be the best.

But what about in our Christian faith? Is there a *best*?

The Bible is clear. We can't earn our way to heaven with good deeds. Our salvation, which is God's gift of eternal life, has *nothing* to do with us and *everything* to do with Jesus. Without Jesus, there is no salvation.[1]

But have you ever wondered if everyone will be equal in heaven? Entry into heaven is only through God's grace, but could the "good deeds" we do in this world impact the *quality* of our afterlife? If we give away our toys, feed the homeless, and read our Bible every day, will we be honored in heaven?

I put the question to Scot. "Will some Christians be rewarded more than others in heaven for the good things they did on earth?" I asked. "Like maybe they'll get a bigger room or walk around wearing a shiny, jewel-filled crown."

Scot had heard of churches teaching about different "levels" of heaven. "I even remember as a kid being motivated to memorize Bible verses because of the rewards I'd get in the form of recognition from teachers," he said to me.

But instead of talking about his experiences or what other Bible experts believed, he brought up a parable told by Jesus in Matthew 20:1–16 that shows how God views rewards.

In the story, an estate owner hires laborers early in the morning to work in his vineyard. He promises to pay each man a denarius, which was the established fair wage for a day's worth of work. Later in the morning, the landowner hires more workers, saying he will pay them "whatever is right." He does this again at noon, in the midafternoon, and at five o'clock in the evening.

When the workday ends, the landowner gives a denarius to the laborers who were hired last and have only worked an hour. The workers who were hired first and labored all day in the hot sun notice what the others are being paid. They expect to get more, since they have done a lot more work. But they are also given a denarius. Instead of being thankful, they start to grumble.

Hearing their complaints, the landowner says, "I am not being unfair to you, friend. Didn't you agree to work for a denarius? Take your pay and go. I want to give the one who was hired last the same as I gave you. Don't I have the right to do what I want with my own money? Or are you envious because I am generous?"[2]

Scot paused from his storytelling and leaned forward. "The landowner's actions are seen as outrageous and even unjust."

*I can see why,* I thought. *Some of the men worked* a lot *longer than others.*

Scot seemed to read my mind. "But God's ways aren't our ways," he continued. "In God's kingdom, the correlation [connection] between work and reward seems out of whack. As humans we're precise in our fairness, but God is lavish. A key line is this: 'Or are you envious because I am generous?' God's generosity is the opposite of human envy. We crave status and position, but he is gracious. In heaven, we'll all be gazing equally at God in *his* glory—not thinking of our own." In other words, everyone who follows and believes in God on earth will get the same amazing reward, and we won't worry about who has what once we're in heaven.

## Crowns, Rewards, and Equality

"But," I asked Scot, "what about passages concerning rewards and 'crowns' that Christians earn in this life?"

I read to him from 2 Corinthians 5:10, which says, "We must all stand in front of Christ to be judged. Each one of us will be judged for what we do while in our bodies. We'll be judged for the good things and the bad things. Then each of us will receive what we are supposed to get."

The Bible talks about several crowns that Christians can receive.

- James 1:12 says the person that keeps going when times are hard and stands up for Jesus Christ will receive the "crown of life." This crown will be given to all followers of Jesus.
- First Thessalonians talks about a "crown of rejoicing,"[3] which appears to be given to someone who tells others about Jesus and helps bring them into God's kingdom.

- Second Timothy 4:8 promises a "crown of righteousness" will be given by God to those who eagerly wait for his return.

"All these verses and examples of crowns make it sound like we can earn status in heaven," I said.

I thought I had a good argument. Scot didn't blink. "All the talk about rewards shouldn't distract us from focusing on God's glory and his promise that we will all experience fulfillment forever in heaven," he said.

As an example, he asked me to read through the apostle John's last visions of heaven in Revelation 20–22, which looks at how people will be judged and what the new heaven and earth will be like.

Once I finished, he said, "There are no gradations [levels or different status] there. Nobody is more important than anyone else. In the final heaven, all God's people will be full of joy. God's generosity will overwhelm any sense of connection between what we did on earth and any reward in the afterlife. In Revelation 4:10, it says the saints will 'lay their crowns in front of the throne.' That's a good picture for us—any crowns deserve to be thrown at the feet of the God of grace."

In other words, our crowns aren't earned or given to bring *us* glory—their ultimate purpose is to be laid at the feet of God to bring *him* glory.

New Testament scholar Craig Blomberg analyzed all the Bible's passages about rewards and concluded, "I do not believe there is a single NT [New Testament] text that, when correctly interpreted, supports the notion that believers will be distinguished one from another for all eternity on the basis of their works as Christians."

Most commentators, Craig said, agree that the texts about crowns "are not at all talking about degrees of reward in heaven but simply about eternal life." He added, "The purpose of Christians standing before God's bar of justice [as described in 2 Corinthians 5:10] is to declare them acquitted [innocent from their sins], not to embarrass them before the entire cosmos for all their failings."[4]

Similarly, many biblical experts don't believe rewards in heaven would involve any sort of visible perk, such as a larger room or different clothes. These would only reduce the joy of others and eternally remind people of their personal shortcomings.

"In the end," Scot summed up, "I see the talk of rewards as being motivational language to encourage us. It certainly motivates me—although, ultimately, shouldn't we joyfully serve God purely out of gratitude for his grace?"

Scot's words struck a chord. The purpose of our good deeds should be to bless others, not build up ourselves. Serving isn't true service if we're doing it to get something in return. That's called selfishness. God calls us to be selfless—to give to others without expecting anything in return.

Speaking of *others* reminded me of my next question. Who will be in heaven? Is it going to be a huge party of just our favorite friends, or a more somber celebration? There was one thing I was certain of: I won't be there all alone.

# Cross-examination

**1.** What motivates you to do your best? (circle your top two)

RECEIVING A REWARD

ENCOURAGING COMMENTS
FROM AN ADULT

POSITIVE PEER PRESSURE

THRILL OF WINNING

IT'S JUST THE RIGHT THING TO DO

Why do the things you circled encourage you to try harder?

**2.** Do you agree with this statement: "The motivation of Christians ought to be to please God, not to strive for rewards in heaven"? Why or why not?

**3.** Do you think everyone will be treated the same in heaven, or do you believe some Christians will be rewarded more than others? Is that fair? What does that say about God?

# WHO WILL BE IN HEAVEN?

# 9

When Jesus lived, he didn't act like everyone thought he would. He ate with sinners, walked with those who were sick, and hung out with the poor. He treated everyone with kindness and love . . . except for many of the religious leaders.

The Pharisees and scribes knew God's laws and taught them in the temple. They were supposed make it easier for people to grow closer to God. Instead, they made it harder. They were proud of following their rules—613 in all! They liked to look holy and put on a religious show so the people would see how "good" they were.

Jesus saw right through them. He knew that in their hearts they followed rules, not God. Instead of praising the good deeds they thought would get them into heaven, Jesus called the Pharisees "pretenders" who shut the door of the kingdom of heaven in people's faces.[1]

Jesus came to open the door into heaven, not shut it. He talked about following two commands—love God and love others—not about obeying more than six hundred rules. He said everyone who believes in him will have eternal life.[2]

With all of this in mind, I asked Scot what I thought would be a simple and straightforward question: "Who will be in heaven?"

"That's easy," he said. "The Bible says it clearly: *Jesus*."

"I know that," I replied. "But how do people get there?"

"Ah," Scot said, "that's the way we tend to look at things, right? We want to know what we have to do to get into heaven. And the answer, again, is Jesus. When we put the focus on *us* and what *we* need to do to get to heaven, we take our attention away from *him*. We don't *do* anything to get into heaven—we don't have to practice a lot of religious rituals or live up to a long list of demands or accomplish a bunch of good deeds. We simply have to look to Jesus, turn to him, believe in him, and let *his* life, death, and resurrection be *our* life, death, and resurrection."

I saw his point. Instead of asking, "How do I get to heaven?", we should be asking ourselves, "Am I in Christ?"

Scot went on to explain it this way. "Everything begins with Jesus. So the answer is, those who are *in Christ* will be in heaven. Heaven is for Jesus and his people."

## The Gospel Is the Good News

Scot's logic was convincing. It also meant that Jesus is the only way into God's kingdom—a claim that upsets many people. If the word *gospel* means "good news," that doesn't sound like good news to them. *There must be other ways*, they think.

Many other religions teach that people earn their way to heaven through good deeds. But just like with the

Pharisees, that puts the emphasis on created laws—not the Creator's laws.

God made everything, and he gets to make the rules. Christianity is the only religion that teaches we can't do anything to earn our way into heaven. It's all about Jesus and his love and sacrifice for us.

When I thought about all my past mistakes and failures—and even some present ones—that *did* sound like good news, so I asked Scot, "How would you explain the gospel?"

Scot took a deep breath. "Well, we need to look at what the New Testament specifically calls the gospel. In 1 Corinthians 15, Paul says *this* is 'the gospel' and 'by this gospel you are saved'—namely, 'that Christ died for our sins according to the Scriptures, that he was buried, that he was raised on the third day according to the Scriptures, and that he appeared to Cephas [Peter] and then to the Twelve.' *That's* the gospel."[3]

Scot explained that the earliest Christians shared the gospel by telling the story of Jesus. He was the promised Messiah, God's Son, coming down to earth. He died unjustly at the hands of sinners. God overturned his death and raised him back to life. He ascended into heaven, and he's coming back one day in the future to rule.

The gospel hasn't changed. So when we talk to people about how they can go to heaven, we shouldn't focus on how we will be happy when we die.

Scot said in conclusion, "We should focus on the story of Jesus. It's a redeeming story. Through it, we encounter the hero to this greatest true tale ever told. We meet the one who loves us so much that he endured the cross to pay for our sins."

## What about the Babies?

I couldn't argue with his conclusion that the gospel is what matters, but it did bring up a question: What about people who never hear the gospel? If they don't know Jesus is the only way to eternal life or don't have the chance to make a decision—like a baby who dies—will they go to heaven?

So I asked Scot, "What does the Bible say about children who die before they can understand the truth about Jesus?"

"The Scriptures don't come right out and explicitly say what happens to infants or children," he said. "When you piece together the clues—not just some verses, but the overarching teachings about God's nature—many theologians conclude that, yes, they will be in heaven."

In support of that belief, many Bible scholars point to Romans 1:20, which declares that unbelievers are without excuse because of the evidence for God in creation. Young children, on the other hand, don't experience creation as adults do. Therefore, they can't logically be held accountable for failing to draw the conclusion that God exists.

Other Christian thinkers believe in the salvation of children because of what David says in 2 Samuel 12. In this passage, one of his wives had just given birth to a son who became ill. David stopped eating and cried out to God for mercy. When the baby died after seven days, David said, "Someday I'll go to him. But he won't return to me." In other words, David was saying, "I'll see my son again in the afterlife, but he's not coming back to this world."

Jesus also gave some hints about who might be in heaven. In Matthew 19:14, he says, "Let the little children come to me. Don't keep them away. The kingdom of heaven belongs to people like them." And in Luke 18:17, God's Son says, "What I'm about to tell you is true. Anyone who will not receive God's kingdom like a little child will never enter it."

While these verses don't prove children who aren't able to hear about Christ and make a decision will go to heaven, they do show God has a special place in his heart for little kids.

"So what's your position?" I asked Scot.

"I start with the fact that God is loving, good, and just," he said, "which leads me to conclude that God wouldn't send infants or young children into eternal darkness. Of course, we don't know for sure. But I believe in an expansive heaven, where these children will grow to full maturity and flourish for eternity."

## Heaven and Its Alternative

I'd been talking with Scot for hours, and we'd covered a lot of ground. His words and insights carried a lot of hope. In heaven, families will be reunited. Children who had never been born, through miscarriage or other circumstances, could meet their brothers and sisters and parents. We'll celebrate, sing, explore, and never be bored in a glorious re-creation of our world. And at the center of heaven, on the throne, exalted and lifted high, will be Jesus Christ—our leader, our Savior, our Lord, our King, our closest Friend, our All in All.

More than ever, I wanted to keep my eyes on Jesus. His story alone points the way to eternal life.

I walked out of that stone church after my interview with Scot and sat alone in my car for quite a while. All of this talk of heaven was so uplifting. Sadly, I knew other ways lead to a dead end.

As unsettling as it is, I couldn't avoid the subject of hell. I picked up my cell phone. It was time to get on another plane. This time I was going to Florida, so I could talk with one of the few philosophers who could bring a balanced biblical perspective to a very dark topic.

**1.** When you hear that "heaven is for Jesus and his people," what's your immediate reaction? (circle one)

**THAT'S NOT ME.     THAT'S THE GOOD NEWS!          WHY IS GOD SO
                              CLOSED-MINDED?**

Explain your answer.

**2.** Are you encouraged by what Scot said about babies who die—without ever having the opportunity to accept Jesus as Savior—going to heaven? How does that support the idea that God is loving, good, and just?

**3.** Jesus said in John 14:6 that he is the only way to heaven. Do you agree with this claim? Why do you think Jesus used the words that he did?

# IS HELL FOR REAL?

Hell is scary.

Maybe that's why hell is a topic we don't like to talk about . . . or even think about.

And if we do think about it, our thoughts quickly turn ghastly. While kids often picture heaven as full of beauty and light and horses and fun, hell looks *very* different.

When asked about their thoughts about hell:

- Sarah, age ten, imagined hell is filled with bad creatures and fire everywhere. In her mind, it's all red and orange and yellow—really hot!
- Christian, age nine, said he thinks hell will be underground, like all dark and red. And it'll be hot, with volcanoes always erupting.
- Rooban, age eight, pictured hell filled with cats. You know, because cats are evil.[1]

Instead of thinking about hell, most people just deny it exists. It's out of sight and out of mind. And on the off chance that hell does exist, they think they certainly won't be going there.

Research shows most people believe they'll go to heaven when they die (more than six out of ten). Only two out of a *hundred* think they'll end up in hell.[2]

That's certainly not what Jesus taught. Jesus spoke more about hell than anyone else in the Bible. He referred to it as a scary, hopeless, everlasting place of judgment. In Matthew 7:13–14 (NLT) he said, "The highway to hell is broad, and its gate is wide for the many who choose that way. But the gateway to life is very narrow and the road is difficult, and only a few ever find it."

The Bible is clear about the existence of hell, but it's less descriptive about what hell will be like. Under Christianity's traditional teaching about hell, it's a place of pure evil—filled with weeping and wailing, flames and flailing, darkness and dread. While that's horrifying, it's not the worst part. In hell, people will spend an eternity separated from God.

So how does Scripture describe the fate of people who refuse to accept God's free offer of salvation?

To find that answer, I traveled to a place of great heat— the Atlantic coast of Florida. While certainly not as hot as hell, it was very warm when I visited Paul Copan, a professor of philosophy at Palm Beach Atlantic University. Paul is a rigorous scholar who has edited or authored nearly forty books and spoken around the world about the truth of the Christian faith.

## Flames, Darkness, and Gnashing of Teeth

Paul wrote about hell in one of his most recent books, *Loving Wisdom: A Guide to Philosophy and Christian Faith.* That's where I began our conversation.

"In your book, you say the belief in hell has troubled both believers and unbelievers alike," I began.

"Yes, it has," Paul replied.

He pointed to great Christian thinkers who have said they would love to discard the doctrine of hell but couldn't. As followers of Christ, we can't pick and choose which bits of the Bible to believe and which to reject. All of it is God's Word, therefore all of it is truth. The Bible says the judge of all the earth will do what is right (Genesis 18:25). And throughout history, God has proven his goodness and justice.

"The doctrine of hell can remind us that there is an accountability before God," Paul explained. "Jesus said to repent or perish. The consequences of separating ourselves from him are, indeed, dire and miserable."

But how miserable? I wondered. God is good and just. He made heaven to reward those who follow him. From the images that we see of hell in movies, cartoons, and paintings, maybe it isn't that bad. After all, a funny-looking guy wearing a red costume and holding a pitchfork doesn't seem too scary.

"How can we sort out what's biblical and what isn't?" I asked. "That seems to be getting harder because churches don't talk much about hell."

Paul explained that in current times some teachers and leaders are trying not to make people feel uncomfortable. In attempting not to offend anyone, they stay away from using words or ideas people don't like. And people don't like to think about hell.

"Well, nobody enjoys thinking about being consumed by eternal flames," I added. "Do you think the fires of hell are literal flames?"

"I don't believe hell is a place of intense thermal output," Paul answered, meaning the flames are symbols meant to show us how awful it will be.

He noted that many Bible scholars have made the point that if two key images of hell were taken literally—flames and darkness—they would cancel each other out. The fire would bring light into hell.

I raised my hand to stop him. "I get that," I said. "But isn't the idea that flames are a metaphor a modern attempt to soften the picture of hell for people who are scared by it?"

Paul shook his head, noting that a metaphor always points toward a reality that it's trying to illustrate.

"Both images—flames and darkness—represent existence away from the Lord's presence," Paul said. "This is the real essence of hell: being cut off from our source of life and joy and being separated from God's blessings forever. Darkness evokes this sense of separation and removal. The reference to flames represents severe, holy judgment. To be away from the presence of the Lord is the worst loss possible for any human being."

"What about references to gnashing of teeth?" I asked. "Seven times in Matthew and Luke, these words are used to describe hell."

"New Testament scholar Craig Blomberg says this reflects anger at God," Paul said from his research. "For example, those who were about to stone Stephen to death in the book of Acts were gnashing their teeth in anger."[3]

"So you're saying people in hell are so hostile toward God that they wouldn't *want* to be in heaven?" I asked.

"Right. They would have to repent in order to be in God's holy presence," Paul said. "The gnashing of teeth is meant to warn us that hell is spiritual misery. Those in hell would be much more content in their own self-absorbed misery away from God rather than face the discomfort of God's glorious presence."

## God Doesn't Send Anyone to Hell

Next, I asked a question that so many people use to challenge the biblical teachings about hell. "Why would a good God send people to hell?" I said.

Paul looked at me. "I think that question is framed incorrectly."

"How so?" I asked.

"The operative word is *send*," he pointed out. "Each choice we make in this life moves us closer to our ultimate destination—whether toward or away from God. We set our own spiritual and moral compasses. Thus, those who reject God *send themselves* to hell. Humans choose to separate themselves from God and hand over themselves to hell—and God reluctantly lets them go."

"But isn't allowing never-ending torment in hell inconsistent with God's loving character?" I said.

Paul explained that everlasting hell is a fair consequence for those who deliberately reject an infinite God, who's infinitely good.

"Your see," he said. "they have spurned the knowledge of God and the boundless gift of salvation he offers. God is most concerned with the direction of a person's heart. People aren't condemned to be away from God because they committed a string of sins, but because they spurned the greatest Good." In other words, God would like everyone to choose salvation, but those who decide not to believe and receive that gift—and actively live their lives away from God—will spend eternity separated from him.

Theologian Denny Burk put it this way: Sinning against an infinitely glorious being like God is an infinitely heinous offense that is worthy of an infinitely heinous punishment. Too often, we have a diminished view of our sin—and as a result, the judgment due for it—because we have a diminished view of God.

But endless punishment in hell isn't accepted by all Christian scholars. Paul also brought up Revelation 20:10–15. In this passage, it says the devil and his minions will be thrown into the lake of fire where they will "suffer day and night for ever and ever" (v. 10). Then Death and Hell will give up their dead and anyone whose name is not written in the book of life will be thrown into the lake of fire (v. 15).

While nearly all Bible scholars agree the devil and his demons will suffer forever, some say humans who were in hell will be snuffed out during this "second death" (v. 14). These scholars point out that angels and humans are very different created beings. The devil and demons are former angels who were cast out of heaven for rebelling against God. They were eternal life-forms from the start, so their punishment will never end. But these scholars argue that God's final judgment will end the punishment for people who rebelled against God by refusing to accept his gift of salvation. These people will cease to exist after being thrown into the lake of fire.

But no matter how these verses in Revelation are interpreted, Paul emphasized the apostle Paul's words that "each person is judged according to his deeds."[4]

"As I said earlier," Paul continued, "the Bible asks, 'Will not the Judge of all the earth do right?' And the answer is, yes, of course he will. In hell, the degree of misery will be correlated to the degree of responsibility."

In other words, a serial killer and a self-absorbed Hollywood star who turned up his nose at God won't experience hell in the same way.

"Human beings will not get away with evil but will be held accountable for their actions—and that's a good thing," Paul said.

To make his point, Paul told a story about Romanian pastor Richard Wurmbrand. Richard and his wife, Sabina, rescued Jewish children out of ghettos during WWII. After the war, Richard was thrown into prison and tortured for his faith under the new Communist government. Communism claimed there was no God. Christian churches were closed. Richard didn't back down from his beliefs in the midst of persecution. He spoke out boldly about the truth of Jesus Christ.

As I thought about what I knew about Richard Wurmbrand, Paul paged through some notes to find Wurmbrand's words. "He wrote, 'The cruelty of atheism is hard to believe. When a man has no faith in the reward of good or the punishment of evil, there is no reason to be human. There is no restraint from the depths of evil that is in man. The Communist torturers often said, "There is no God, no hereafter, no punishment for evil. We can do what we wish."'"[5]

## A Dreadful Torment

Of course, we can't do what we wish. God will judge our deeds. The evil, unrepentant men who tortured Richard

Wurmbrand and countless others will suffer the consequences of their actions when they die.

"So hell is a well-deserved torture chamber," I said.

Again, Paul paused to correct the wording of my statement. "There's a difference between *torture*, which is externally imposed, and *torment*, which is internally generated. Torment is self-inflicted. It's because people have resisted the grace of God that they end up having their own way forever. God doesn't torture. He isn't willing that any perish; hell is the result of humans freely separating themselves from him and his love."

"Can you describe the nature of the torment in hell?" I asked.

"Revelation 14:11 speaks of 'the smoke of their torment' and that they have 'no rest day or night' forever," Paul explained. "To be tormented means not being at rest. Just two verses later, we see that this torment is the opposite of the 'rest from their labor' that's experienced by faithful saints."

Everything about hell sounded dreadful. I guess that's why Jesus used metaphorical language about flames and worms and gnashing teeth. Literal descriptions just can't convey the horrors of hell; it's far worse than anyone can envision.

As we took a break in our conversation, I thought about Jesus' parable of Lazarus and the rich man. In it, God's Son uses the imagery of fire to give a harrowing peek at an afterlife separated from God.[6] Lazarus, a beggar, is safely embraced by Abraham after his death. But the ungenerous rich man is "in torment," pleading for Lazarus to "dip the tip of his finger in water and cool my tongue, because I am in agony in this fire." A chasm prevents that. The rich man begs for Lazarus to warn the man's five brothers "so that they will not also come to this place of torment." Abraham replies that they should listen to the prophets.

Granted, the focus of the parable isn't to actually teach about the afterlife. This is a story not about eternal hell, but about the intermediate state between death and the final judgment.

Nevertheless, Jesus would never mislead about the ultimate fate of the unrepentant. It would make sense that the imagery he used would portray a foretaste of the suffering that awaits those in hell.

Bestselling Christian author Randy Alcorn wrote, "In his story of the rich man and Lazarus, Jesus taught that in Hell, the wicked suffer terribly, are fully conscious, retain their desires and memories and reasoning, long for relief, cannot be comforted, cannot leave their torment, and are bereft of hope."[7]

Talk about bleak, and yet . . .

What if all of humanity were to personally benefit from God's kindness and desire for everyone to be redeemed?

Paul had offered a strong case for the traditional view of hell. The Bible showed it was a real place filled with real people who disobeyed God's commands and turned their backs on his offer of forgiveness.

Now I wondered how Paul would handle the increasingly popular notion of *universalism*—after all, a God of love would certainly want everyone to be saved.

**1.** Have you ever heard a pastor talk about hell? If so, did it make sense to you? What emotions did you feel?

**2.** After reading this chapter, if you were to tell a friend about hell, what are some of the points you would want to emphasize?

**3.** Why is it important to understand the difference between *torture* and *torment*? Is God a torturer?

**4.** Paul said God doesn't *send* people to hell, but that people "who reject God *send themselves* to hell." Does this distinction make sense to you? Why or why not?

# DOESN'T GOD WANT EVERYONE IN HEAVEN?

**11**

What's the coolest part about castles?

Alligator-filled moats are pretty awesome. So are stone towers guarded by brave knights, ballrooms packed with dancing princes and princesses, and amazing food served in a great hall. But the coolest parts of castles may be the secret passageways.

Secret passageways were built into nearly every castle throughout history. A fake fireplace might lead to a stairway for escape. Or pull on a specific book on a shelf in the library and it reveals a hidden room.

In the same way that castles have secret passageways, some people want to believe there's a secret entrance into heaven. Or at least a hidden back door that people can sneak through.

Although Jesus said, "I am the way" and, "No one comes to the Father except through me," they convince themselves that a loving King of kings would want everyone in his kingdom. Makes sense, right?

Some Bible teachers like this idea so much that they reject the finality of hell. They say God will forgive all people in the end. Maybe unrepentant sinners might spend a little time in hell as punishment for not turning to Jesus for forgiveness, but ultimately, we all live forever in heaven. This idea is known as *Christian universalism.*

I wanted to quiz Paul to see whether this view makes any biblical sense.

## Will All Be Saved?

Christian universalists emphasize God's overarching narrative of creation, the fall, then Christ reconciling everything—and everybody—to himself.

They cite verses such as:

- Titus 2:11—"God's grace has now appeared. By his grace, God offers to save all people."
- John 12:32—"And I am going to be lifted up from the earth. When I am, I will bring all people to myself."
- 1 Corinthians 15:22—"Because of Adam, all people die. So because of Christ, all will be made alive."
- 2 Peter 3:9—"The Lord . . . doesn't want anyone to be destroyed. Instead, he wants all people to turn away from their sins."

In recent decades, there has been an uptick in interest in Christian universalism. After all, it seems so nice and inclusive. I asked Paul what he thought, and his answer was firm.

"I believe universalism is a dangerous doctrine," he said flatly. "You certainly get no hint of it in the Old Testament, where Psalm 1:6 reads, 'The LORD watches over the lives of godly people. But the lives of sinful people will lead to their death.'"

Paul admitted it's natural for us to want everyone to be saved. It's a terrible thought to think a beloved family member or best friend might not be in heaven.

"Even God desires it!" Paul declared, his eyes widening. "As 1 Timothy 2:4 and 2 Peter 3:9 say, he wants all to come to a knowledge of the truth. But Christ is the *potential* Savior of all, not the *actual* Savior of all. Salvation is offered to all, but not all freely accept it."[1]

"What about the Bible's use of the word *all* to describe those who are ultimately redeemed," I asked, "as in 1 Timothy 2:6, which says Jesus 'gave himself to pay for the sins of all people'?"

"We need to examine the word *all* closely," Paul said. "For example, when the gospel of Mark says 'all the people from Jerusalem' flocked to be baptized by John, the author doesn't mean every single individual was doing that. It simply meant a lot of people. In this case, Jesus did pay for all the sins of the world and made grace available to all sinners, but we have to accept that payment on our behalf if we're going to benefit from it. Not everyone will do that."

## The Freedom to Say No

God doesn't force his love on people. That's a fact I discovered during my own journey to become a Christ follower. Jesus' own teaching indicates that some will embrace him while others will not—a point that he makes in the parable of the four soils in Matthew 13.

In that example, Jesus said people respond differently after hearing the truth of God's love and forgiveness. Some believe deeply in their hearts right away. They grow into strong Christians, telling others about the good news they received. From this one strong "seed," hundreds of people come to believe the truth. Other people, Jesus said, "quickly fall away from the faith" after accepting the truth. They never grow "roots" either because they never truly believed or because they failed to grow deeper in their faith through prayer and reading the Bible. Still others hear the truth but hang out with people who argue against God's Word. They worry what their friends will think, so they choose not to follow God. And the last group of people totally reject God's message from the start.

"We routinely read in Scripture that God does his utmost to reach people, only to be rebuffed," Paul continued. "In Matthew 23, Jesus weeps over Jerusalem, longing to gather the city as a hen gathers her chicks, but Jerusalem refused. In Acts 7:51, before he was stoned, Stephen accuses his stiff-necked persecutors of always resisting the Holy Spirit. For stubborn rebels, the more God pours out his grace, the more they want to flee. They want to find happiness on their own terms."

That reminded me of what Paul and I had talked about earlier. Some people are so hostile toward God that they wouldn't even *want* to be in heaven. They want to do what they want, when they want, to whom they want—without any consequences. But that's not the way life works. Breaking God's rules has consequences, on earth and in the afterlife. In order to live forever in heaven, every person must choose to receive the free gift of forgiveness and eternal life offered by Jesus.

Paul had already built a strong case against universalism, but I asked him to conclude with any other reasons why this view falls short biblically. He did have more reasons. Lots of them.

"Both the Old and New Testaments reveal the opposite of universalism," Paul began, listing off several verses.

- The contrast between the righteous and unrighteous is shown in Psalms, Proverbs, and Daniel 12:2 (NIV), which talks about those awakening to "everlasting life" and others to "shame and everlasting contempt."
- In the New Testament, there's the judgment of the sheep and goats (Matthew 25:31–16).
- John 3:16 indicates there's a difference between those who have "eternal life" and those who "die."
- In Revelation 13:8, we find a limited, fixed number of names written in the Lamb's "book of life"—and a person has to be included in that book in order to be in the presence of God.
- In Romans 9:3, the apostle Paul wished he could be condemned so that his Israelite brothers and sisters could be saved.

I could tell that Paul was prepared to go on, but in my mind the case was closed on universalism. Sure, maybe it's the way many people wish heaven could be. But God has been clear from the start of history. He is holy. Sin, evil, or any type dishonesty can't be allowed in heaven. It's only the rescuing and cleansing power of Jesus that enables anyone to be in God's presence.

God loves everyone, died for everyone, and desires for everyone to be with him for all eternity. But he gives each person the freedom to say no. We can accept his forgiveness, or we can reject the love he showed for us by dying for our sins on the cross.

So where does all of this leave us? Back with the traditional view of heaven and hell. And knowing the truth of heaven and hell should motivate us to tell as many people as we can that there *is* indeed a judgment, but there is also a divinely designed escape route through Jesus. Through Jesus' death and resurrection, God freely offers the gift of eternal life to everyone who will receive it in repentance and faith.

Hell can't be erased. Heaven is for real.

Hell is a hard truth, but it's not the *only* truth in Scripture. Since the beginning of my journey, I'd become even more grateful that Jesus is *the* truth. And it's through him that the gates to heaven are open to us.

My case for heaven was nearly closed, but there was still a big area to be explored. What do followers of other religions believe happens after *they* die? Not everybody believes in Jesus. So what evidence exists that Christianity is the best option?

One scholar's name jumped to mind who was singularly able to shed light on that question. It was time to book a ticket back to the Midwest. But this time I'd be going to Indiana.

**1.** After reading this chapter, how would you describe the differ-ence between Christ being the *potential* Savior of all but not the *actual* Savior of all?

**2.** The Bible says Jesus came to "look for the lost and save them" (Luke 19:10). Based on what you've read so far, how successful was Jesus in this mission? Put on X on the line that best describes your opinion.

| 1 | 5 | 10 |
|---|---|---|
| Total failure | Sort of successful | Mission accomplished |

Explain why you placed your X where you did.

**3.** If someone who does not believe in Jesus asked you directly, "Am I going to hell?", how would you respond to them in order to give them the truth and hope?

# WHAT DO OTHER RELIGIONS SAY HAPPENS AFTER DEATH? 12

More than 7.5 billion people live on earth. That's a lot of people. Each person follows a belief system that guides his or her decisions and actions. Even atheists, who don't believe in any gods or religion, put their faith in something—usually science or their own abilities.

Researchers say there are hundreds of religions around the world. That's a lot. But only three of these belief systems have more than one billion followers.

With nearly 2.4 billion believers, Christianity is the world's largest religion. Islam ranks second at just under 2 billion followers. Hinduism is the third largest religion on the planet with 1.1 billion followers.[1]

Just like any thorough look at heaven requires a dive into hell, it's important to understand what other religions teach about the afterlife. Does Jesus' claim of being "the way and the truth and the life," stand up when tested against other belief systems? How do Christianity and Islam differ in their beliefs of heaven and hell? And why is the Hindu idea of reincarnation having such a profound impact around the world?

Getting to the truth would require some deep thought and an honest look at the evidence. But before I got there, I had to establish some facts about the world's largest religions.

## What Does Islam Say?

Islam began around A.D. 600. According to tradition, Muhammad of Arabia was visiting a cave near Mecca in modern-day Saudi Arabia. The angel Gabriel appeared before the forty-year-old and told Muhammad that he was a prophet of Allah—the Islamic people's deity. The angel gave him a message. Muhammad wrote down the teachings, which become the Qur'an—or the Muslim holy book. Muhammad said the message he received was directly from Allah.

Muslims, or followers of Islam, follow strict rules. They must pray memorized prayers five times a day at certain hours. Many times these prayers are recited out loud in a mosque, which is a Muslim church. Muslims have many rules about what they can and cannot eat. For instance, they are prohibited from eating pork or drinking alcohol.

Islam is based on five pillars. Muslims believe in a creed that says there is no god but Allah. In addition to praying five times a day, they must recite other ritual prayers. In addition, Muslims are required to give money to the needy, fast from sunrise to sunset during a certain month each year, and make a trip to Mecca (their holy city) at least once in their lifetime if they are physically able.[2]

Muslims do believe in life after death. By following rules and doing good deeds, a Muslim earns his or her way into heaven, which they call Jannah. Salvation is through works. Going to the mosque, learning the Qur'an, and being good parents are some of the actions that help get a person into paradise. Muslims have no guarantee of heaven and don't know where they'll spend eternity until after they die. That's because they believe two angels will question them after their death. If the angels determine a person was a good rule-follower and did more good than bad, then he or she is admitted into paradise.[3]

In Islam, Jannah is often described as a garden, flowing with rivers of pure water, milk, wine, and clear honey. Families are reunited. People wear beautiful clothes and eat delicious foods forever and ever. Jannah has extra benefits for men in Islam. Between seventy and one hundred women attend to a man, providing for his every desire.[4] These same promises are not made to women.

Hell, or Jahannam, is the place for wrongdoers. Those who don't believe in Allah will enter hell, where they will be tormented and punished. The Qur'an describes gruesome images of hell where fire burns the faces of disbelievers until their lips peel off. They drink boiling water that shreds their guts. Then they grow new skin and repeat the agony.[5]

Islamic hell has various levels with a different severity of punishment in each level. Muslims who didn't take their faith seriously or made fun of the reality of a Judgment Day will be in Jahannam. Of course, so will murderers, those who stole money from orphans, idol worshipers, and the prideful.[6]

## What Do Hindus Believe?

Hinduism may be the world's oldest religion. It's hard to date back, because it's not a single religion but a combination of different traditions and philosophies. Historians say Hinduism was formally developed in India around 1,500 B.C. from the combined teachings of many cultures. These teachings were written into a book called *The Vedas*.

Hindus worship up to 300 million gods. The central god, Brahman, is god over all the others. Worship services are held at a temple, but individual shrines are also set up in Hindu homes. Followers burn incense, put up pictures or physical representations of gods, and pray at these shrines.

One of the key beliefs of Hinduism is *atman*, or the existence of a soul. Hindus think the soul exists forever. Instead of going to heaven or hell when a person dies, followers of Hinduism believe the soul is reincarnated.[7]

*Merriam-Webster Dictionary* offers this definition of reincarnation: "rebirth in new bodies or forms of life, *especially*: a rebirth of a soul in a new human body."[8] Most forms of reincarnation include animals as well. In Latin, the word *reincarnation* literally means "to come again in the flesh."

In Hinduism, the ultimate destination of the soul isn't paradise. Rather, salvation is "becoming one" with Brahman by cleansing yourself of bad deeds through doing good deeds. If a person does more good than bad, they reincarnate to a higher-level being. The opposite is also believed to be true. If a person does more bad than good, they are reincarnated into a lower being, such as a bird or a bug. After many lives, the goal is to stop coming back in different life-forms and unite with the "ultimate soul."

Another fundamental belief of Hinduism is the law of karma, which is a kind of moral cause and effect. There's good karma and bad karma. Doing good deeds builds good karma. Bad behaviors result in bad karma. Meditation helps a lot in building good karma. Hindus believe the more a person meditates—which includes breathing deeply while focusing their minds and then repeating one word or phrase over and over, called a mantra—the purer his or her soul becomes.

Hindus also follow strict rules about what they can eat. Beef and pork are prohibited. In fact, the cow is a scared animal for them. For this reason, many Hindus are vegetarians.[9]

## Pyramid to Heaven

Researchers say Islam will surpass Christianity as the world's largest religion by 2060.[10] The belief in reincarnation has also had a profound impact worldwide. This belief system has shown up in subtle—and not so subtle—ways in children's books, movies, and entertainment.

Much of what you've read in this book so far makes up the foundation of Christianity. If Christianity is true, you might conclude that the Bible's teachings automatically rule out reincarnation. And you'd be correct. In Christianity, there are no do-overs. As Hebrews 9:27 says, "People have to die once. After that, God will judge them." And what about Islam? Its heaven looks very different than the Christian view. The heaven of the Bible is a paradise filled with peace, joy, and praising God. Heaven in the Qur'an can seem more enjoyment-based—especially for men—than spiritual.

So I wanted to know: With so many different theories about an afterlife in various religions, why should people trust what Christianity teaches about the world beyond? I needed to find an expert who had carefully studied other religions and come to a reasoned conclusion.

Immediately, Chad Meister's name came to mind. Early

in his life, Chad had been influenced by Hinduism, New Age philosophies, and other teachings. At that point, he didn't know whether to believe in Allah or Brahman or some other divine reality.

As he got older, Chad began to seek answers, carefully analyzing different worldviews. *Which is reasonable? Which is logical? Which is livable? Which one has evidence on its side?*

Chad says he started by asking the question, "What is truth?"

He ended up researching worldviews for a year and a half. At the end, his conclusion was clear: Christianity is the most reasonable, the most livable, and the best supported by evidence.

Today, Chad is the chair of the religion and philosophy department at Bethel University in Mishawaka, Indiana. He's also a highly respected and widely published scholar of more than twenty books. I wanted to discuss Chad's first book, *Building Belief: Constructing Faith from the Ground Up*. In it, he builds what can be called the "heaven pyramid." This visual depiction demonstrates how the building blocks for the truth about Christianity are built on a firm foundation.

I sat down with Chad in his office at the university and asked him to take me on a journey to the top of the pyramid.

## Level 1: Truth

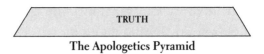

The Apologetics Pyramid

Some people say all religious claims are true. That sounds very considerate and accepting, but it's logically absurd.

"All major religions make truth claims that are absolute," Chad explained. "And yet they fundamentally contradict each other. Our task is to discover what's true and what isn't."

Because different religions assert opposite beliefs, all religions can't be true. For example, the Bible says Jesus is the Messiah, who gave his life as a sacrifice for sin. Other religions deny this claim. Both beliefs *can't* be true.

The foundation of the pyramid is truth. And truth isn't relative. That is, it can't be determined by what we *believe*. Truth is whatever is *consistent with reality*. Simply put, truth is truth. To figure out what is truly true, we must continue to climb the pyramid.

## Level 2: Worldviews

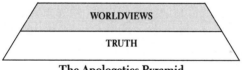

The Apologetics Pyramid

The next layer of the pyramid examines the three major worldviews.

"A worldview is a collection of beliefs and ideas about the central issues of life," Chad said. "It's the lens through which we view the world. Broadly speaking, every religion or ideology can be found within one of three worldview categories—*theism*, *atheism*, or *pantheism*. But, of course, their core assumptions contradict each other, and therefore only one can be true."

Chad said we should break down each worldview by asking five fundamental questions:

1. Is there a God, and what is God like?
2. What is ultimate reality?
3. How is knowledge obtained?
4. Where is the basis of morality and value found?
5. Who are we as human beings?

He started with theism, or belief in a personal God. The major theistic religions—Judaism, Christianity, and Islam—claim there is one God, creator of all, who is all-knowing, all-powerful, all-present, and all-good.

"The ultimate reality in theism is God, who is beyond the physical realm of existence," Chad said. "We acquire knowledge through our five senses and other means, including the revelation in Scripture. The basis of morality is God. Right, wrong, good, evil—they're all based on the nature of an infinite God who created everything. Finally, what does it mean to be human? We're not on a par with God, though we're on a higher plane than the rest of the animal kingdom. We're unique, and we have an immaterial soul that lives on in eternity."

Next, Chad talked about atheism, which means disbelief in God or gods. In this worldview, nothing exists beyond the physical world. There is no heaven or hell or spiritual world. Since the physical world is all that exists, knowledge can only be gained through observation, logic, and the scientific method. Morality is subjective. In other words, it can vary from place to place and time to time. There is no absolute standard. Finally, humans are just electromechanical machines—animals that have grown in complexity over billions of years thanks to evolution.

Chad concluded with pantheism, which has both

philosophical and religious aspects to it. "Generally speaking, pantheism is the belief that all is one, and all is god—or Brahman in Hinduism. Animals, plants, insects, rocks, you, me—everything is one and the same ultimate reality." If you're a fan of Star Wars, you might recognize this as being similar to *the force*. Chad continued, saying, "Knowledge is acquired not through rational inquiry but through meditation, chanting, and other practices intended to empty the mind." Good and evil are an illusion. In pantheism, humans are god. We have spiritual divinity because we are one with the universe.

I let all this soak in for a few moments. "Three worldviews—all contradictory to each other," I said. "How can anyone determine which is true?"

Chad proposed two tests for which worldview is most plausible: *logic* and *livability*. A worldview is false if its core beliefs are internally contradictory or incoherent. Also, a worldview should be rejected if it cannot consistently be lived out.

That sounded reasonable to me, so he started with atheism.

"First, there's the logical problem of good," Chad said. "If there's no objective morality, the atheist can't logically declare that there are such things as objective good, evil, right, or wrong. Atheists can't even really claim that the murder of innocent children is morally evil. They could say they're offended by it, but that's a preference—not a moral standard."

Chad concluded since objective moral values *do* exist, then atheism must be false. On top of that, atheism fails the livability test. If morality is relative, objective beliefs—such as the value of human life—become void. Without universally accepted truths, chaos would rule as everyone did whatever they wanted . . . including kill each other.

"What about pantheism?" I asked.

"Pantheists have a problem with right and wrong as well," Chad said.

He told me about having a spaghetti dinner with a pantheist, who told him, "Everything is God and everything is one. There are no distinctions."

Chad replied to her, "But if there are no distinctions, then there is ultimately no right and wrong, no distinction between cruelty and noncruelty, or between good and evil." With that, he took a pot of boiling water from the stove and pretended he was going to spill it on her. "Are you *sure* there's no distinction between right and wrong, cruelty and noncruelty?" he teased.

She quickly agreed there did seem to be a practical distinction between right and wrong that must be lived out for society to exist.

"Besides," Chad added, "pantheism seems to be logically incoherent. In pantheism, I am God and ultimately impersonal. Yet I'm encouraged to discover this fact about myself. If God is the changeless 'All', I can't be changeless and at the same time change in order to realize that I am changeless."

Now my head was spinning, but I saw his point.

"So," I said, "your bottom line is that pantheism and atheism are disqualified because of logical contradictions, incoherence, and unlivable claims, but theism survives your tests."

"Correct," Chad responded. "There's so much more to be said, and I've written a lot on this. But my conclusion is that, given all of this, theism in general—and Christianity in particular—is the most plausible worldview."

## Level 3: Theism

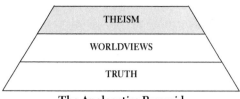

The Apologetics Pyramid

I was interested in Chad's assessment of the positive evidence for theism. Certainly a creator God who decides the rules would make a livable system of set laws that allows people to thrive. But what about logical reasoning? I offered him a challenge: "Give me three reasons that theism is true."

"Just three?" Chad replied with a smile. "Okay, sure. First, there's the fine-tuning of the universe. A life-permitting universe is extremely unlikely. Scientists have discovered that if you were to slightly alter any of the basic constants of physics, it would make life impossible. There are fifty or more examples from physics that are calibrated on a razor's edge so that life can exist. The probability of this occurring by undirected natural causes or chance is virtually zero."

I was familiar with the scientific evidence that an organized universe and a life-giving Earth couldn't have come about by chance evolution. Just like Chad, I've written numerous books that provide clarify for Christian beliefs, including *The Case for Christ Young Reader's Edition* and *Case for a Creator for Kids*.

"Okay, what's your second argument for theism?" I said.

"The beginning of the universe points powerfully toward a Creator," Chad replied. "Virtually all scientists now agree the universe began to exist at some point in the past. Therefore, the universe must have a cause. Given that *universe* means time, space, matter, and physical energy, this cause must itself be timeless, spaceless, matterless, and powerful enough to create all the physical energy that exists. That describes God."[11]

"All right, what's your third reason for theism? I said.

"It's the moral arguments I raised earlier regarding atheism and pantheism," Chad said. "First, if there are objective moral values, then God exists. Objective moral values are precepts that are universally binding on all people at all times and places, whether they follow them or not. Second, we know that objective moral values *do* exist—for example, it's objectively evil to kill innocent children. Therefore, God exists."

His arguments seemed logical. But several religions believe in theism. That brought us to the next level of the pyramid.

## Level 4: Revelation

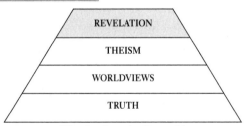

The Apologetics Pyramid

Judaism, Christianity, and Islam believe its scriptures are authoritative and divinely inspired. Christians see no conflict between their Bible and the Jewish Torah. After all, the Jewish scripture *is* the Bible's Old Testament. Both Christians and Jews agree the Old Testament is accurate and authoritative. The difference is that Christians regard Jesus as the promised Messiah and accept the New Testament as God's Word.

On the other hand, there are irreconcilable differences between the Bible and the Qur'an. The Islamic holy book explicitly contradicts teachings about the God of the Bible, the death and resurrection of Jesus, and the teaching that Jesus is God's unique Son. Consequently, if the Christian Bible is reliable and true, it would rule out the validity of the Qur'an, because it contradicts the Bible.

The New Testament contains the starkest contrast with Jewish and Islamic beliefs. Chad proposed three tests for whether it's plausible to believe that the New Testament can be trusted.

"First, there's the bibliographical test," he said, "which refers to whether we can trust the transmission [accurate copying] of the text through history. It's no exaggeration to say the evidence for the New Testament text is staggering."

More than 5,800 ancient Greek manuscripts and fragments of the New Testament are still in existence. Some of these date back to fewer than a hundred years after the originals. That number is far more than other ancient writings. While this doesn't prove that the New Testament is true, it does offer good reason to believe today's Bible is an accurate representation of what was originally written.

"Next," Chad continued, "there's internal evidence. Several New Testament documents refer to their authors as *being* eyewitnesses to the events, *mentioning* eyewitnesses, or *interviewing* eyewitnesses. For example, the author of Luke's gospel talked with eyewitnesses and notes he 'carefully investigated everything' to establish 'the certainty' of what occurred.[12] Peter says he was personally an eyewitness to the events he described.[13]

Paul notes there are hundreds of witnesses to what he claimed about Jesus and his resurrection."[14]

Chad added, "No other religious text has this level of eyewitness authentication. This gives the New Testament special credibility. And then there's external evidence, which looks at whether outside sources provide any corroboration. Over and over again, archaeological discoveries have confirmed—and never disproven—core New Testament references. Plus, there are ancient writings outside the Bible that confirm the basic outline of Jesus' life described in the Bible."

I asked, "Are you saying, then, that the New Testament has been proved as reliable?"

"I'm saying that any reasonable person would be justified in rendering the verdict that the New Testament is essentially trustworthy," Chad said.

And since the New Testament is the most reliable source of truth, it stands alone—above the Qur'an or Jewish Scriptures.

## Level 5: Resurrection

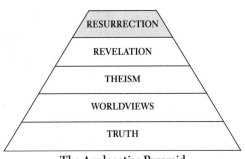

The Apologetics Pyramid

The final category of evidence for Christianity is the resurrection of Jesus, which proved his claim of being the Messiah and God's only Son.

Historian and philosopher Gary Habermas analyzed 2,200 expert sources on the resurrection. Out of this study, he compiled several facts that are considered historically accurate by a large majority of scholars, including skeptics. They are:

1. Jesus was killed by crucifixion.
2. The disciples believed he rose and appeared to them.
3. Jesus' tomb was empty.
4. The church persecutor Saul was converted.
5. The skeptic James, Jesus' half brother, went from doubter to believer.[15]

"I'll focus on just two facts," Chad said. "First, Jesus' tomb was vacant."

This is reported in the gospel of Mark, the first gospel written, which comes too quickly after Jesus' death for an elaborate, legendary story to have developed. In fact, all four gospels report that the tomb was empty.

"And this is highly significant: even Jesus' enemies conceded the tomb was empty," Chad said. "Instead of disputing it, religious leaders and the Roman government tried to explain it away. All they needed to do in order to squelch Christianity was produce Jesus' body, which they never did."

They couldn't because there was no body. Jesus had risen from the dead. Over and over, the evidence is firm that the tomb was vacant.

"Second, Jesus' followers believed that the risen Jesus appeared to them," Chad said. "All four gospels reference this. Peter confirmed that he was an eyewitness to the resurrected Jesus. And Paul reported that he encountered the risen Christ."

This meeting, as described in Acts 9:1–19, transformed Paul from a persecutor of Christians to a follower of Christ. Paul died spreading the truth of Jesus. In fact, his letters to the early churches make up much of the New Testament.

"The most persuasive evidence, though, comes from a letter Paul wrote roughly twenty years after Jesus' death," Chad continued. "In it, he recounts a creed of the earliest Christians that cites groups and individuals who were eyewitnesses to the resurrected Jesus, including five hundred people at once."

Many experts believe this creed, which appears in 1 Corinthians 15, starting at verse 3, was actually formulated within *months* of Jesus' death. Historically speaking, that's a news flash!

I'm personally familiar with *nine* ancient sources, inside and outside the New Testament, that confirm and corroborate the conviction of the disciples that they had encountered the resurrected Jesus. The two sources from outside the Bible report what they learned firsthand from eyewitnesses themselves.

First, there's Clement. The early church father Irenaeus reports that Clement conversed with the apostles, and the writer Tertullian says Clement was ordained by Peter himself. Second, there's Polycarp. Irenaeus says Polycarp was taught by the apostles, and Tertullian confirms that the apostle John appointed Polycarp as a bishop. Both Clement and Polycarp specifically confirm that it was the *actual* resurrection of Jesus that motivated the disciples to spread the Christian faith.[16]

Many historical events are believed to be true because of one or two ancient sources. Jesus' resurrection has nine impressive sources, not to mention a mountain of additional historic evidence!

"The historical facts, in my opinion, are clear and convincing—Jesus rose from the grave, and in doing so, he demonstrated his divine nature," Chad said. "And this clinches Christianity as the worldview that makes the most sense to me. It's plausible and it's livable. As the pyramid demonstrates, it's built on a solid foundation that can be trusted."

## Level 6: The Gospel

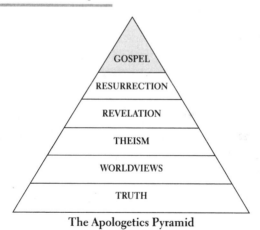

The Apologetics Pyramid

The good news of the gospel is the summit of the pyramid.

"Jesus says he's opening God's kingdom to us," Chad said, quickly summarizing the gospel. "The Bible makes it clear that the kingdom of God is where God rules in a perfect way—he loves his people, provides for them, cares for them—and we gratefully love and serve and worship him in return. He invites everybody to enter—and in his kingdom, we are transformed."

Through logic and evidence, Chad had shown it's thoroughly reasonable to take the Bible's teachings on the afterlife with the utmost seriousness. Which means we can trust Jesus as the most reliable source for truth about what happens after death.

As long-time professor at Denver Seminary Douglas Groothuis said, "We have powerful and persuasive evidence that Christianity is true. If Jesus really is the Son of God who died for our sins, then his account of the afterlife is the most credible of all."[17]

## One True ~~Religion~~ Relationship

I'd begun this chapter wondering what other major religions believed about the afterlife. Chad's unique heaven pyramid had provided a sturdy foundation for trusting what Jesus taught about eternal life. Christianity was unique. It wasn't about following rules; it was about following Jesus. Christianity wasn't a religion; it was a relationship.

In other religions, people try to reach God. In Christianity, God reaches down to mankind to restore relationship. Consider this:

- Jesus promises that anyone in relationship with him will spend eternity with him. With other religions, followers don't know for sure where they're headed until *after* they die.
- Jesus is the only God who died and came back to life.

- Christianity is the only religion where eternal life in paradise is not based on our good deeds, but in Jesus' life-giving sacrifice of dying for our sins to rescue us from the grave.

Through interview after interview, my confidence in heaven had grown. The case for heaven was not based on wishful thinking, make-believe, legend, or mythology. It is the promised glorious future that awaits all who put their trust in Christ.

# Cross-examination

**1.** From what you read in this chapter, how would you describe the differences between Christianity and the other major world religions—Islam and Hinduism?

**2.** Does the "heaven pyramid" make sense to you? Which level of the pyramid was the most important for you and why?

**3.** Why do you think the resurrection of Jesus is the key to Christianity? Since Jesus returned from the dead, what are some of the implications for your life and your future?

# CAN'T I DECIDE WHAT I BELIEVE ABOUT THIS LATER?

# 13

D eath is not the end. There's more after we die.

From the beginning of my quest to figure out what happens after death, I followed where the facts took me. Science might be able to delay death, but technology doesn't hold the keys to eternal life. Death is a certainty. But not a certainty to be feared if a person has a solid faith in Jesus.

The evidence points to heaven being a reality. Jesus has flung open the gates for everyone who wants to enter through repentance and faith in him. Our soul will live on and one day be reunited with an eternal body in the new heaven and new earth. And what an amazing place it will be! Even the most creative artists or out-of-box-thinkers can't imagine the beauty, peace, and love that will surround us.

Bible scholars, like Scot McKnight, can only provide a glimpse of heaven's glory as described in God's Word. Scot did, however, deliver plenty of evidence for why it's reasonable to believe in heaven. He also handed out hope when it comes to the people and pets that might join us in in eternity.

As glorious as heaven will be, hell will be the opposite.

No book about heaven can ignore hell. So I talked to Paul Copan about the stark reality of what it looks like to be separated from God forever.

Finally, I investigated what other major religions believe about the afterlife and came to the logical conclusion that Jesus was—and still is—the most reliable source for information.

The scientific, biblical, historical, and philosophical evidence is there. Heaven is for real.

The simple answer to what happens after death is this: We continue to live. The only thing in doubt is our final residence.

Have you received the gift of forgiveness that Jesus purchased for you on the cross? If so, you will spend forever in his presence in heaven. If not, you must pay for your sins yourself as you spend eternity separated from God in hell.

Throughout all the flights, car rides, interviews, and fast food along the way, one phrase kept constantly ringing in my mind. And it wasn't some philosophical argument, bit of scientific evidence, or eyewitness account. It was the words of my good friend Luis Palau, when I asked him just before he died what message he'd send back from heaven to people who didn't know Christ:

"Don't be stupid."

## Most Important Decision

Right now, you might feel like you have all the time in the world. You're young. You likely feel healthy. Your whole future is in front of you.

Statistics show you can expect to live around eighty years. That's twice as long as people lived during the 1800s.[1] Eighty years may sound like a long time, but compared to eternity it's just a blip.

The Bible calls our time on earth a vapor, saying, "You don't even know what will happen tomorrow. What is your life? It is a mist that appears for a little while. Then it disappears" (James 4:14).

Instead of making plans for future success, it's important to lock in what your future will hold right now. What do you believe about Jesus? Only God knows how long you'll live.[2] Taking a chance with your future is—in the words of Luis Palau—*stupid*.

As Luis pointed out, why would someone pass up the offer of God's grace to pursue an empty life without God? Why would a person turn his or her back on heaven and choose hell? Neither is a smart decision.

To have hope for a bright and glorious future, there's only one answer: it's Jesus.

Heaven means hope. Not a wishful thinking or a cross-your-fingers sort of blind optimism, but a confident hope. For followers of Jesus, who gratefully embrace him as their forgiver and leader, death is merely a doorway to a world of grandeur and wonder, of satisfaction and joy, of flourishing friendships and stimulating experiences, of gazing with gratitude at the face of the Lord and Savior.

Perhaps for you, there's still a hitch in the story about Jesus. You're wondering if God is really fair. If Jesus holds the keys to heaven, what's the fate of people who never get a chance to hear his message of redemption and eternal life? And why is Jesus the only way into heaven? Wouldn't it be fairer if there were other ways to get into heaven?

To answer the last question first, God is always fair.

In fact, he's *more than* fair. God is forgiving, faithful, and patient. Throughout the Old and New Testaments and into modern history, he has provided numerous opportunities, evidences, and miracles to encourage people to turn to him. God consistently delays his rightful judgment and gives second, third, fourth, and fiftieth chances.

And if you think about it, if God didn't give us only one surefire and absolute way to get into heaven, it would lead to all kinds of confusion. God is not a God of confusion. He makes the truth clear: Jesus is the *only* way into heaven.

Each person must make his or her own personal decision to follow Jesus. Heaven is not like the gym. There are no "family passes." In other words, just because your mom, dad, or grandparents are going to heaven, you don't get an automatic ticket. Each of us has to make our own decision to put our trust in God and what his Son, Jesus, accomplished for us on the cross.

But back to the question about the fate of those who never had an opportunity to hear the gospel message. Are they doomed to an eternity in hell? This issue troubled me so deeply that I did hundreds of hours of study, research, and interviews.

What I learned was that God hasn't told us explicitly how he is going to deal with those who don't hear the truth about Jesus before they die. The Bible says, "The LORD our God keeps certain things hidden. But he makes other things known to us and to our children forever."[3]

In other words, some things will be kept secret from us until we get to heaven. But we do know a few things that help us sort through this issue.

First, we know from Scripture that everyone has a moral

standard written on their heart by God and that everyone is guilty of violating that standard.[4] Chad Meister talked about this moral standard in the last chapter. That's why our conscience bothers us when we do something wrong.

Second, we know that everyone has enough information from observing the created world to know that God exists, yet people have suppressed that truth and rejected God anyway.[5] Scot McKnight mentioned this in chapter 9.

Third, both the Old and New Testaments tell us that those who wholeheartedly seek God will find him.[6] In fact, the Bible says that the Holy Spirit seeks after us first, making it possible for us to seek him. This suggests that people who respond to the understanding that they have about God's existence from living in the world and who earnestly seek after the one true God will find an opportunity, in some way, to receive the eternal life that God graciously provides through Jesus.

Sometimes we get a glimpse into how God accomplishes this. One time I met a man who had been raised by Hindu gurus in an area of India where there were no Christians. As a teenager, he concluded there were too many contradictions in Hinduism. Its teachings didn't satisfy his soul. He called out to God for the real truth. In an absolutely remarkable series of events, God brought people into his life who shared the story of Jesus with him. As a result, he became a follower of Christ.

In my book *The Case for Miracles for Kids*, I document example after example of how Jesus is appearing in spectacular dreams to Muslims in countries that are closed to the gospel of Christ. In these dreams, Jesus points people down the path to eternal life with him.[7]

Over and over in Scripture and in current events, we see

that God is incredibly fair. The very first book of the Bible asks, "Won't the Judge of all the earth do right?"[8] The answer to that question is *yes*. Exactly how much knowledge a person has to have about Jesus, or precisely where the lines of faith are drawn, only God knows. He and he alone can expose the motives of a person's heart.

In the end, we can be confident that whenever people—of any race, in any culture, at any time—cry out to God, he will respond, often in stunning and unexpected ways. While we might have questions now, at the end of history each of us will personally marvel at how absolutely perfect God's judgment will be.

So all that needs to be known about this matter is: God is good, God is loving, and God is fair. When we believe those foundational truths, we can trust him for the outcome of each and every person's eternity.

## The ABCs of Faith

As for you and me, the issue of where we'll spend eternity doesn't come down to ignorance of the truth. Even if you had never heard the story of Jesus before, you read it in this book. Over these many pages, you've discovered the evidence and considered the reasoning that supports the truth of Christianity and the existence of heaven.

In a sense, you've been a detective in the case for heaven during the time you've been reading this book. And at some point, a good detective reaches a conclusion.

Maybe the time for that is now. The pathway to paradise may be narrow, but it's not confusing. It's as easy as ABC.

*A=Admit.* Admit you have sinned. The Bible says everyone has sinned.[9] You've lied, acted selfishly, gotten angry, and broken God's laws. Agree with God that your sins make you unholy. Acknowledge that you haven't always followed God's rules and there's no amount of good deeds that could get rid you of your guilt.

*B=Believe.* Believe that Jesus died on the cross to pay the penalty for your sins. The only reason God's Son came to earth was to sacrifice his life for yours. Jesus lived a perfect, sinless life and took the punishment you deserved. Only he can rescue you from sin, make you holy, and restore your relationship with God.

*C=Choose.* Choose to give your life to God. Belief is a choice. Faith is a choice. By choosing to accept God's free gift of forgiveness, your eternal life in heaven is guaranteed.

For me, it took years of investigating the claims of Christianity before I admitted that I had sinned, believed that Jesus paid the price for my sins, and chose to pray and accept Jesus as my Savior.

One of the very first verses I memorized as a new follower of Christ was 1 John 5:13 (NIV): "I write these things to you who believe in the name of the Son of God so that you may *know* that you have eternal life" (italics added).

As a result of my decision to follow Jesus, I knew that I had eternal life. Then over the years, God transformed my character, morality, values, worldview, attitudes, relationships, and priorities—for the better.

How about you? Do you want to know that you have eternal life? All you need to do is say a sincere prayer, like this one:

Dear God,

I know I am a sinner. Thank you for sending your Son, Jesus Christ, to die on the cross for my sins. I believe Jesus rose again from the dead and lives with you today in heaven. I choose to turn away from my sinful ways and follow you. Thank you for your love and forgiveness. And thank you for changing my life forever. Amen.

If you just prayed that prayer, tell somebody. Share that you just made the most important decision of your life to be "in Christ." Your faith in God isn't something to hide; it's something to celebrate. You are God's child for all eternity! You will dwell with God, and he will dwell with you—in the new heaven and the new earth.

And know this: Your decision to follow Christ doesn't just change your eternity, it will change the rest of your life on this earth too.

## Cross-examination

1. As you finish this book, where are you on your spiritual journey on a scale of 1–10? Put an X on the line where you rate yourself.

   | 1 | 5 | 10 |
   |---|---|---|
   | Don't believe in God | Just came to Christ | Fully faithful to God |

   Did your number change from the beginning of the book? Why do you think that happened?

2. After reading this chapter, do you think God is fair about who gets to live forever in heaven and who does not? Why?

3. Do know in your heart and mind that you will spend eternity with God in heaven? If so, memorize 1 John 5:13: "I write these things to you who believe in the name of the Son of God so that you may know that you have eternal life." Write down the evidence that supports your knowledge of this truth.

**4.** If you're not a follower of Christ, what additional evidence would you need to believe in Jesus? Remember, you don't have to know *everything* to know *something*. If the evidence discussed in this book is convincing, is there any reason why you wouldn't receive Jesus right now as your forgiver and leader through a prayer of repentance and faith?

# HOW CAN I REALLY LIVE FOREVER?

# 14

As humans, we want to live forever.

It's implanted in us. As we learned in chapter 6, the Bible says God has "set eternity in the human heart."[1] We desire to understand eternity and how our lives fit into it.

Billionaires try to buy more time on earth or create digital realities where they will never die. Other people strive for fame to give them a kind of *symbolic immortality.*

When kids in Great Britain were asked what they wanted to be when they grew up, the top answer wasn't a firefighter, veterinarian, teacher, or police officer. More than any of those careers, kids simply wanted to be "famous."[2]

And it's not just kids. Adults also seek fame, often in ridiculous ways. One man earned his way into the *Guinness Book of World Records* by breaking forty-six toilet seats with his head in one minute. That might have earned him a headline (and a headache), but he was quickly forgotten when a different person accomplished an equally bizarre feat . . . for example, the guy who put fifty-two socks on his right foot in sixty seconds.

The truth is, the quest for fame seldom succeeds in the long term.

## Symbolic Immortality

Apart from a belief in Jesus, there's no way to live forever. During my conversation with Clay Butler Jones from the first chapter, he described many ways people pursue symbolic immortality. Since they know they can't physically live forever, they look to leave a legacy or make an impact on the world so their memory will be kept alive. This can be done by conquering an empire, building a temple, writing a book, establishing a family, accumulating a fortune, or exceling at numerous other things.[3]

One of the most common ways of pursuing symbolic immortality is having or adopting children. Since a family's name gets passed down through children, it's an obvious way to be remembered.

When I asked Clay if living on through your kids worked, he answered with a question of his own. "Do you know the first names of your great-great-grandparents?" he asked.

I felt sheepish. "Uh, no, I guess I don't."

Clay patted my shoulder. "Don't feel bad," he said. "I often ask classrooms full of students if they know the first names of their great-great-grandparents—and so far only one student has said yes. So much for trying to keep yourself alive through your family."

"What about creating something of lasting value?" I asked. "People paint masterpieces, put their names on a building, or start a website to be remembered."

"That doesn't always turn out well," Clay said. "This kind of fame can be rather fleeting."

Buildings get renamed or torn down, paintings lose their luster or get ruined, popular websites and online platforms get replaced. In the mid-2000s, Myspace was the largest social media website in the world. Today, it'd be difficult to find a single teenager who knows who founded that once-popular platform.

## Living in Light of Heaven

Human schemes for immortality will always fail. We will be forgotten. That's the bad news.

The good news is that Jesus won't be. God's Word will never pass away. Jesus' name and fame will grow throughout eternity. The sooner we live in that reality, the greater impact we can have on this planet.

There's nothing symbolic about it. What we do for God lasts forever. A lasting legacy doesn't come through buildings, kids, careers, wealth, or fame. It comes through serving and living for Christ.

Jesus' original disciples figured that out. As they wholeheartedly followed God's Son, their mission, their attitudes, their relationships, and their priorities were all turned upside down and inside out. They started as an easily forgotten group of fishermen, a tax collector, and a sort-of politician. They became an unstoppable and unforgettable force for truth.

The firsthand knowledge that Jesus performed miracles, died for sins, rose from the dead, and ascended into heaven changed the disciples' lives *and* the history of the world.

What about you and me? How can our lives change *today* in light of heaven? Since Jesus' life leads us to our heavenly home, shouldn't we dig deeper into his teachings and commit to applying his wisdom to our everyday lives? Knowing that we will someday inherit the riches of heaven, shouldn't we stop clinging to the earthly possessions that take our attention away from what's really important? As we anticipate a paradise of eternal pleasures, shouldn't we refrain from mindless pursuits that only bring fleeting enjoyment and sometimes leave lasting regret?

Jesus told his followers to not gather riches on earth where they can be lost, stolen, and destroyed by moths and rats. "Instead," he said, "gather for yourselves riches in heaven."[4] These treasures last forever.

Jesus doesn't want us to love possessions; he wants us to love people. When we treat people with kindness, comfort a hurting friend, forgive someone who hurts us, or share the love of Jesus, we store up treasures in heaven.

And we don't have to wait for heaven to see the impact we can have! The apostle Paul told the early church to live like they're already there. He said "we are citizens of heaven" whose Savior is the Lord Jesus Christ (Philippians 3:20). Paul used the image of a "colony of heaven" to inspire the people to live out their faith on earth.

As a Christ follower, you might feel like a minority in your school and around your neighborhood. But you possess a power that has changed the world and continues to change people's lives.

Heaven is a place of perfect peace, joy, and love. You act like you're already in heaven by being an example as you repair relationships and ask for forgiveness from somebody you've wronged. When you boldly represent the ideals of your faith through your actions, you become a light to the world and can have an eternal impact.

And even if people forget you, here's the best news of all: God remembers what we do for him—forever.

That's my final challenge to you. Refuse to be satisfied with the fact you're going to heaven, and try to take as many people with you as you can.

Grace has been given. The party has started. The admission has been paid. Eternity is in the balance. Seek God. Trust him. Follow him. And live out the hope you have of heaven right now.

# Cross-examination

**1.** Do you have a desire for your name to be remembered after your death? What's the best way for that to happen? (Circle best answer/answers.)

BECOME RICH                    HELP THE LESS FORTUNATE

GET FAMOUS                      TELL PEOPLE ABOUT JESUS

PAINT AN AMAZING PIECE OF ART

**2.** What was your reaction to the fact very few people know the first names of their great-great-grandparents? Do you know yours? If not, find out and learn more about their lives. Write down what you discover.

**3.** What do you want written on your tombstone, as a way for people to remember something about you? Can you put it in a sentence or two?

# SCRIPTURE SPEAKS

## Some of My Favorite Verses Dealing with Heaven

### Psalm 16:9–10

So my heart is glad. Joy is on my tongue.
    My body also will be secure.
You will not leave me in the place of the dead.
    You will not let your faithful one rot away.

### Psalm 23:4, 6

Even though I walk
    through the darkest valley,
I will not be afraid.
    You are with me.
Your shepherd's rod and staff
    comfort me. . . .
I am sure that your goodness and love will
    follow me
        all the days of my life.
And I will live in the house of the LORD
    forever.

## Psalm 84:10

A single day in your courtyards is better
    than a thousand anywhere else.
I would rather guard the door of the house of
    my God
        than live in the tents of sinful people.

## Psalm 116:3–4

The ropes of death were wrapped around me.
    The horrors of the grave came over
me.
    I was overcome by sadness and sorrow.
Then I called out to the Lord.
    I cried out, "Lord, save me!"

## Isaiah 11:6 (NIV)

The wolf will live with the lamb,
    the leopard will lie down with the
goat,
the calf and the lion and the yearling together;
    and a little child will lead them.

## Isaiah 65:17

"I will create new heavens and a new earth.
    The things that have happened before
will not be remembered.
    They will not even enter your minds."

## Daniel 6:26-27

"He is the living God.

He will live forever.

His kingdom will not be destroyed.

His rule will never end.

He sets people free and saves them.

He does miraculous signs and wonders.

He does them in the heavens and on

the earth."

## Matthew 6:19-21

"Do not gather for yourselves riches on earth. Moths and rats can destroy them. Thieves can break in and steal them. Instead, gather for yourselves riches in heaven. There, moths and rats do not destroy them. There, thieves do not break in and steal them. Your heart will be where your riches are."

## Matthew 25:21 (NIV)

"His master replied, 'Well done, good and faithful servant! You have been faithful with a few things; I will put you in charge of many things. Come and share your master's happiness!'"

## Luke 23:42–43

Then he said, "Jesus, remember me when you come into your kingdom." Jesus answered him, "What I'm about to tell you is true. Today you will be with me in paradise."

## John 14:2–4

"There are many rooms in my Father's house. If this were not true, would I have told you that I am going there? Would I have told you that I would prepare a place for you there? If I go and do that, I will come back. And I will take you to be with me. Then you will also be where I am. You know the way to the place where I am going."

## Romans 6:23 (NIV)

For the wages of sin is death, but the gift of God is eternal life in Christ Jesus our Lord.

## Romans 8:18

What we are suffering now is nothing compared with our future glory.

## 1 Corinthians 2:9

It is written that
"no eye has seen,

no ear has heard,
and no human mind has known."
God has prepared these things for
those who love him.

## 1 Corinthians 15:42–44

It will be like that with bodies that are raised from the dead. The body that is planted does not last forever. The body that is raised from the dead lasts forever. It is planted without honor. But it is raised in glory. It is planted in weakness. But it is raised in power. It is planted as an earthly body. But it is raised as a spiritual body. Just as there is an earthly body, there is also a spiritual body.

## 1 Corinthians 15:54–57

What does not last will be dressed with what lasts forever. What dies will be dressed with what does not die. Then what is written will come true. It says, "Death has been swallowed up. It has lost the battle."

"Death, where is the victory you thought you had?

Death, where is your sting?"

The sting of death is sin. And the power of sin is the law. But let us give thanks to God! He gives us the victory because of what our Lord Jesus Christ has done.

## 2 Corinthians 5:1

We know that the earthly tent we live in will be destroyed. But we have a building made by God. It is a house in heaven that lasts forever. Human hands did not build it.

## 1 Thessalonians 4:13–14

Brothers and sisters, we want you to know what happens to those who die. We don't want you to mourn, as other people do. They mourn because they don't have any hope. We believe that Jesus died and rose again. When he returns, many who believe in him will have died already. We believe that God will bring them back with Jesus.

## 2 Timothy 4:7–8

I have fought the good fight. I have finished the race. I have kept the faith. Now there is a crown waiting for me. It is given to those who are right with God. The Lord, who judges fairly, will give it to me on the day he returns. He will not give it only to me. He will also give it to all those who are longing for him to return.

## 1 John 5:11

Here is what God says about the Son. God has given us eternal life. And this life is found in his Son.

## Revelation 3:5

"Here is what I will do for anyone who has victory over sin. I will dress that person in white like those worthy people. I will never erase their names from the book of life. I will speak of them by name to my Father and his angels."

## Revelation 7:16–17

"'Never again will they be hungry.
        Never again will they be thirsty.
The sun will not beat down on them.'
        The heat of the desert will not harm
        them.
The Lamb, who is at the center of the area
        around the throne,
        will be their shepherd.
'He will lead them to springs of living water.'
        'And God will wipe away every tear
        from their eyes.'"

## Revelation 21:1–5

I saw "a new heaven and a new earth." The first heaven and the first earth were completely gone. There was no longer any sea. I saw the Holy City, the new Jerusalem. It was coming down out of heaven from God. It was prepared like a bride beautifully dressed for her husband. I heard a loud voice from the throne. It said, "Look! God now makes his home with the people. He will live with them. They will be his people. And God himself will be with them and be their God. 'He will wipe away every tear from their eyes. There will be no more death.' And there will be no more sadness. There will be no more crying or pain. Things are no longer the way they used to be."

He who was sitting on the throne said, "I am making everything new!" Then he said, "Write this down. You can trust these words. They are true."

## Revelation 21:23–26

The city does not need the sun or moon to shine on it. God's glory is its light, and the Lamb is its lamp. The nations will walk by the light of the city. The kings of the world will bring their glory into it. Its gates will never be shut, because there will be no night there. The glory and honor of the nations will be brought into it.

## Revelation 22:4–5

They will see his face. His name will be on their foreheads. There will be no more night. They will not need the light of a lamp or the light of the sun. The Lord God will give them light. They will rule forever and ever.

# ABOUT THE AUTHORS

## Meet Lee Strobel

Atheist-turned-Christian **Lee Strobel** is a former award-winning legal editor at the *Chicago Tribune*. His more than forty books have sold millions of copies. He is also founding director of the Lee Strobel Center for Evangelism and Applied Apologetics at Colorado Christian University (Strobelcenter.com), where students can study online for a bachelor's or master's degree, or just for their own growth.

The *Washington Post* described Lee as "one of the evangelical community's most popular apologists." He received his journalism degree from the University of Missouri and his Master of Studies in Law degree from Yale Law School. Lee was a journalist for fourteen years at the *Chicago Tribune* and other newspapers, winning Illinois' highest honors for both investigative reporting and public service journalism from United Press International.

After probing the evidence for Jesus for nearly two years, Lee became a Christian in 1981. He was later a teaching pastor at three of America's largest churches and hosted the national TV program *Faith under Fire*.

In 2017, Lee's story was depicted in an award-winning motion picture, *The Case for Christ*. He has won numerous national awards for his books, which include *The Case for Christ, The Case for Faith, The Case for a Creator, The Case for Grace, In Defense of Jesus,* and *The Case for Miracles*.

Lee and Leslie have been married for forty-nine years. Their daughter, Alison, is a novelist, and their son, Kyle, is a professor of theology. They have four grandchildren.

## Meet Jesse Florea

***Jesse Florea*** is a bestselling author who has written or edited more than thirty-five books, including *The Case for Miracles for Kids* and *The Case for Grace for Kids* with Lee Strobel. His other books include the *Defend Your Faith Bible,* an apologetics Bible for kids, and *The One Year Devos for Sports Fans*. He has worked at Focus on the Family for over twenty-five years. For most of that time, he's been the editor of Focus' children's magazines *Clubhouse* and *Clubhouse Jr*. He cohosts the "Official Adventures in Odyssey" and the "Official Average Boy" podcasts and speaks at Christian writers' conferences around the country.

Jesse earned bachelor's and master's degrees in communications from Wheaton College, IL, while minoring in biblical studies. He was a high school sports reporter for nearly thirty years, ultimately being inducted into the Colorado High School Coaches Hall of Fame for media. He lives with his wife, Stephanie, in Colorado Springs and enjoys hanging out with his two grown children, their spouses, and his grandchildren.

# NOTES

## Introduction: How Can We *Know* There's a Heaven?

1. Caryle Murphy, "Most Americans believe in heaven . . . and hell," Pew Research Center, November 10, 2015, at www .pewresearch.org/fact-tank/2015/11/10/most-americans -believe-in-heaven-and-hell.

2. Tracy Munsil, "AWVI 2020 Survey: 1 in 3 U.S. Adults Embrace Salvation Through Jesus; More Believe It Can Be 'Earned,'" *American Worldview Inventory*, August 4, 2020, at www.arizonachristian.edu/blog/2020/08/04/1-in-3-us -adults-embrace-salvation-through-jesus-more-believe-it -can-be-earned.

## Chapter 1: Can We Live Forever?

1. Ashlee Vance, "Elon Musk Unveils Brain Computer Implanted in Pigs," *Bloomberg News*, August 28, 2020, at www. bloomberg.com/news/articles/2020–08–28/elon-musk -to-unveil-neuralink-brain-computer-implanted-in-pigs?utm _source=knewz.

2. Zoë Corbyn, "Live for ever: Scientists say they'll soon extend life 'well beyond 120,'" *The Guardian,* January 11, 2015, at www.theguardian.com/science/2015/jan/11/-sp-live-forever -extend-life-calico-google-longevity.

3. Ibid.

4. See Acts 4:12.

5. See Luke 22:54–62.

6. Luc Ferry, *A Brief History of Thought: A Philosophical Guide to Living*, trans. Theo Cuffe (New York: Harper, 2010), 12.

7. Zygmunt Bauman, *Mortality, Immortality, and Other Life Strategies* (Stanford, CA: Stanford University Press, 1992), 31.

8. Clay Jones, *Immortal: How the Fear of Death Drives Us and What We Can Do About It,* (Eugene, OR: Harvest House, 2020), 139.

## Chapter 2: Is Death Something to Fear?

1. Natasha Daniels, "Child Therapist's List of Top Worries by Age," AnxiousToddlers.com, at www.anxioustoddlers.com /worries-by-age/#.YE-b0x17mV5.

2. See 2 Corinthians 5:8.

3. See Romans 2:4.

## Chapter 3: Do We Have a Soul?

1. Jesse Bering and David Bjorklund, eds., "The Natural Emergence of Reasoning about the Afterlife as a Developmental Regularity," *Developmental Psychology* 40 (2004), 217–233, referenced in: Mark C. Baker and Stewart Goetz, eds, *The Soul Hypothesis*, 3.

2. BibleGateway.com search of the word *soul* in the NIrV translation.

3. Quote from Lee Strobel's *The Case for a Creator: A Journalist Investigates Scientific Evidence That Points Toward God* (Grand Rapids: Zondervan, 2004), 261.

4. J. P. Moreland, *The Soul: How We Know It's Real and Why It Matters* (Chicago: Moody, 2014), 71.

5. Sharon Dirckx. *Am I Just My Brain?* (London: Good Book, 2019), 131.

## Chapter 4: Can We Peek into Life Beyond Death?

1. True story compiled from: John Burke, *Imagine Heaven* (Grand Rapids: Baker Books, 2015). Also Beth Ann Krier, "A Step Toward the Light: Research Raises New Questions

About Children's Near-Death Experiences,'" *Los Angeles Times,* September 18, 1990, at www.latimes.com/archives /la-xpm-1990–09–18-vw-815-story.html. And Nancy Ross-Flanigan, "Life After Death," *Chicago Tribune,* October 27, 1992, at www.chicagotribune.com/news/ct-xpm-1992–10 –27–9204070573-story.html.

2. "Girl survives sting by world's deadliest jellyfish," *Daily Telegraph* (London), April 27, 2010.

3. For a full report on Ian McCormack's experience, see: John Burke, *Imagine Heaven,* 139–141.

4. John Burke, *Imagine Heaven,* 326.

5. John Burke, *What's After Life?* (Grand Rapids: Baker, 2019), 5–7. Also see: "Mary NDE" at: www.nderf/experiences /1mary_nde.html.

6. Jeffrey Long with Paul Perry, *Evidence of the Afterlife: The Science of Near-Death Experiences* (New York: HarperCollins, 2010), 72–73.

7. J.M. Holden, "Veridical Perception in Near-Death Experiences," in Janice Miner Holden, Bruce Greyson, and Debbie James, *The Handbook of Near-Death Experiences: Thirty Years of Investigation* (Santa Barbara, CA: Praeger, 2009), 185–211.

8. Jeffrey Long with Paul Perry, *Evidence of the Afterlife,* 44, quoted in John Burke, *Imagine Heaven,* 41.

## Chapter 5: What Is Heaven Really Like?

1. See Luke 23:43.
2. See Acts 7:55.
3. See Revelation 21–22.
4. See Exodus 33:20
5. See 1 Corinthians 15:42-49.

## Chapter 6: Why Should I Believe in Heaven?

1. "Ask Away," Focus on the Family *Clubhouse* magazine, November 2020, page 29. Named changed to protect privacy.

2. N. T. Wright, *Simply Good News* (New York: HarperOne, 2015), 99.

3. See Isaiah 25:6–10; 26:19; Hosea 6:1–2; Ezekiel 37; Daniel 12:2–3. Scot McKnight said to me: "In God's providence and in the unfolding of revelation and redemption, we only learn about a new life beyond death in the final sections of the Old Testament, the prophets."

4. See Rodney Stark, *What Americans Really Believe: New Findings from the Baylor Study of Religion* (Waco, TX: Baylor University Press, 2008), 69–74.

5. Maggie Fox, "Fewer Americans Believe in God–Yet They Still Believe in Afterlife," *NBC News*, March 21, 2016, at www.nbcnews.com/better/wellness/Fewer-american s-believe-god-yet-they-still-believe-afterlife-n542966.

6. Ecclesiastes 3:11, NIV

7. C. S. Lewis, *Mere Christianity* (New York: HarperOne, 1952), 136–137.

## Chapter 7: Will There Be Pets in Heaven?

1. See Revelation 21:18–20, 23.

2. Richard J. Mouw, *When the Kings Come Marching In* (Grand Rapids: Eerdmans, 2002), 20–21.

3. Stanley Brandes, "The Meaning of American Pet Cemetery Gravestones," *Ethnology* 48, no. 2 (Spring 2009).

4. Jessica Pierce, "Do Animals Experience Grief?" *Smithsonianmag.com*, August 24, 2018, at www.smithsonianmag.com/science-nature/do -animals-experience-grief-180970124/.

5. See Alan W. Gomes, *40 Questions About Heaven and Hell* (Grand Rapids: Kregel Academic, 2018), 257. See also Genesis 1:30; Leviticus 24:18; Ecclesiastes 3:19; and Revelation 8:9.

6. Peter Kreeft, *Everything You Ever Wanted to Know About Heaven* (San Francisco: Ignatius Press, 1990), 45–46.

## Chapter 8: Will There Be Rewards in Heaven?

1. See Acts 4:12.
2. NIV translation
3. See 1 Thessalonians 2:19, NKJV.
4. Quotes taken from Craig L. Blomberg, "Degrees of Reward in the Kingdom of Heaven?" *Journal of the Evangelical Theological Society* 35, no. 2 (June 1992): 160, 163, 167, www.etsjets.org/files/JETS-PDFs/35/35-2/JETS_35-2_159-172_Blomberg.pdf.

## Chapter 9: Who Will Be in Heaven?

1. See Matthew 23:13.
2. See John 3:14–15.
3. See 1 Corinthians 15:1–5, NIV

## Chapter 10: Is Hell for Real?

1. Connie Esch, "Kids Describe What They Imagine Hell Is Like," BuzzFeed.com, September 10, 2018, at www.buzzfeed.com/connieesch/kids-from-different-religions-explain-hell.
2. "*AWVI 2020* Survey: 1 in 3 U.S. Adults Embrace Salvation Through Jesus; More Believe It Can Be 'Earned,'" at www.arizonachristian.edu/blog/2020/08/04/1-in-3-us-adults-embrace-salvation-through-jesus-more-believe-it-can-be-earned.
3. See Acts 7:54, NIV.
4. See Romans 2:6.
5. Richard Wurmbrand, *Tortured for Christ* (Colorado Springs, CO: David C. Cook, 50th anniversary edition, 2018), 52.
6. See Luke 16:19–31, NIV.
7. Randy Alcorn, *Heaven* (Carol Stream, IL: Tyndale, 2004), 25–26.

## Chapter 11: Doesn't God Want Everyone in Heaven?

1. "This is why we work and try so hard. It's because we have put our hope in the living God. He is the Savior of all

people. Most of all, he is the Savior of those who believe"
(1 Timothy 4:10).

## Chapter 12: What Do Other Religions Say Happens After Death?

1. "Religion by Country," World Population Review, at
   worldpopulationreview.com/country-rankings/religion
   -by-country.

2. Bernard Lewis and Buntzie Ellis Churchill, *Islam: The
   Religion and the People* (Upper Saddle River, NJ: Wharton
   School Publishing, 2009), 13–19.

3. "How does a Muslim get to Heaven/Major way of Getting
   to Jannah," Quran Reading, March 21, 2018, at www
   .quranreading.com/blog/how-does-a-muslim-get-to
   -heaven-major-ways-of-getting-to-jannah/.

4. "Concept of Heaven and Hell according to Islam," Quran
   Reading, March 29, 2018, at www.quranreading.com/blog
   /concept-of-heaven-and-hell-according-to-islam/.

5. Bernard Lewis and Buntzie Ellis Churchill, *Islam: The
   Religion and the People*, 195.

6. "Concept of Heaven and Hell according to Islam."

7. "Hinduism," History.com, September 30, 2019, at
   www.history.com/topics/religion/hinduism.

8. www.merriam-webster.com/dictionary/reincarnation.

9. "Hinduism," History.com.

10. Michael Lipka and Conrad Hackett, "Why Muslims are
    the world's fastest-growing religious group," Pew Research
    Center, April 6, 2017, at www.pewresearch.org/fact-tank
    /2017/04/06/why-muslims-are-the-worlds-fastest-growing
    -religious-group/.

11. Some physicists have speculated that the universe has
    expanded and contracted eternally, in an ongoing cycle,
    and thus lacks a beginning. But Alexander Vikenkin,
    director of the Institute of Cosmology at Tufts University,
    rules out this and other efforts to posit a beginningless
    universe, saying: "All the evidence we have says that the

universe had a beginning." See Alexander Vilenkin,
*Many Worlds in One: The Search for Other Universes* (New
York: Hill and Wang, 2006), 176. Also see Lisa Grossman,
"Why Physicists Can't Avoid a Creation Event," *New Scientist*,
January 11, 2012.

12. See Luke 1:1–4.
13. See: 2 Peter 1:16.
14. See 1 Corinthians 15:3–8.
15. Gary R. Habermas and Michael R. Licona, *The Case for the Resurrection of Jesus* (Grand Rapids: Kregel, 2004). Also, see my interview with Licona (PhD, Pretoria) in Lee Strobel, *In Defense of Jesus*, 106–164.
16. Lee Strobel, *In Defense of Jesus* (Grand Rapids: Zondervan, 2007), 124.
17. Lee Strobel, personal interview with Douglas Groothuis for research for *The Case for Heaven*.

## Chapter 13: Can't I Decide What I Believe About This Later?

1. Max Roser, Esteban Ortiz-Ospina, and Hannah Ritchie, "Life Expectancy," OurWorldinData.org, October 2019, at ourworldindata.org/life-expectancy.
2. See Job 14:5 and Matthew 6:17.
3. See Deuteronomy 29:29.
4. See Romans 2:15.
5. See Romans 1:20.
6. Jeremiah 29:13 (NIV): "You will seek me and find me when you seek me with all your heart." Hebrews 11:6: "God . . . rewards those who earnestly seek him."
7. Lee Strobel, *The Case for Miracles for Kids* (Grand Rapids: Zondervan, 2018), 87–98.
8. See Genesis 18:25.
9. See Romans 3:23.

## Chapter 14: How Can I Really Live Forever?

1. See Ecclesiastes 3:11, NIV.

2. "Quarter of children want to be 'rich' and 'famous,' finds survey," Premier Christian News, August 6, 2014, at premierchristian.news/en/news/article/quarter-of-children -want-to-be-rich-and-famous-finds-survey.

3. Sam Keen, "Foreword," in Ernest Becker, *The Denial of Death* (New York: Free Press, 1973), xiii.

4. See Matthew 6:19–21.